The Allotment Cookbook

The Allotment Cookbook

PETE LAWRENCE

WEIDENFELD & NICOLSON

First published in Great Britain in 2016
by Weidenfeld & Nicolson, an imprint of
the Orion Publishing Group Ltd
Carmelite House, 50 Victoria Embankment
London EC4Y 0DZ
An Hachette UK Company

10 9 8 7 6 5 4 3 2 1

Text © Pete Lawrence 2016
Design and layout © Weidenfeld & Nicolson 2016

A CIP catalogue record for this book is available from the British Library.

ISBN: 978 0 2978 7109 5

Design by Bryony Clark
Illustrations by Nici Holland

Printed and bound in Germany

The Orion Publishing Group's policy is to use papers that are natural, renewable
and recyclable products and made from wood grown in sustainable forests.
The logging and manufacturing processes are expected to conform
to the environmental regulations of the country of origin.

www.orionbooks.co.uk

For more delicious recipes, features, videos
and exclusives from Orion's cookery writers,
and to sign up for our 'Recipe of the Week'
email visit **bybookorbycook.co.uk**

Follow us @bybookorcook   @bybookorbycook

Find us   facebook.com/bybookorbycook

CONTENTS

Introduction

By day, I work with some of the world's finest chefs and cooks. Then, to relax, I indulge my culinary passion, by growing fresh produce on the allotment; experimenting with my own concoctions in the kitchen; and writing about the results. In truth, whether I'm at work, allotment, or keyboard, I think about food for much of my day. In that I am truly fortunate, yet always hungry.

By contrast to my day job in television, growing veg is the antithesis of stress. The allotment is where I go to escape a busy life and seek inspiration. It is my sanctuary. I often find myself spending long periods just looking at things on the plot. To make me sound even weirder, the more time I spend there, the closer I become to my crops. Not, I hasten to add, in an emotionally unstable way; I simply understand their virtues and finer qualities. I hesitantly suggest that 'relation-ship' is not too big a word. In simple terms, the way I cook and think about food has changed since I have grown my own veg. I feel I appreciate their true value and have a connection with the land. Both are easy to lose in our demanding and busy lives.

We live in a world of convenience. In foodie terms, gastro-nomic heaven is never far away. When you are late home from work on a cold, dark winter's evening, it's understandable that the lure of supermarket fluorescents often proves irresistible in the quest for culinary inspiration. Aisles of juicy red tomatoes, bags of pre-washed salad leaves, asparagus, peppers and vegetables galore all shout, 'eat me now'! Together they are a colourful (though increasingly costly) reminder that when it comes to ingredients, we really can have them all.

Yet for me, this is an illusion. Either our food has enough air miles to qualify for entry to the VIP lounge, or it has been grown under such controlled conditions that it lacks soul or flavour. I am not against supermarkets. They are vital for many. It's just me – I come out in a mental cold sweat at the very thought of supermarket shopping; the noise, congestion and mayhem of negotiating trolleys and queuing for the checkout fills me with dread. I'd rather be on the allotment with my cabbages.

I have three other motivators for digging in the rain. First, growing veg is infinitely cheaper than buying them. I am increasingly shocked by the price of food. It really doesn't cost much to plant a few seeds and the results are worth every penny. Growing food in one or two pots on the windowsill will easily recoup your costs and also soothe your soul. Secondly, I'm conscious that we all need to eat less meat. Since I have immersed myself in the world of vegetable growing, I have found that I rarely miss meat – and when I do eat it, I appreciate it in a way I never did before. I also delight in the taste and texture of vegetables far more than previously. The final driver for me is waste. Perhaps if we all grew a little, used our ingredients more wisely and appreciated the provenance of our food, we might go some way towards living a little more sustainably than we do now.

For me, growing veg feels right. When you hum the same tune as nature – get into its rhythm – then you will learn to savour produce at its very best. If you nod to the seasons you will always find inspiration and your taste buds will enjoy flavour combinations full of vibrancy and vitality. I also believe that eating seasonally is good for the soul. I'm convinced it helps our bodies to adapt to the way nature changes around us. This basic philosophy keeps me focused on those days when the very idea of standing in a howling wind with a fork and a wheelbarrow seems completely absurd.

It takes commitment to brave November winds or February frosts. However, it is such solitary work done on the darkest of days that pays dividends in the long term. Patience is paramount. There is a sizeable gap between the period when most of the work is needed and the time when the reward comes. The truth is that spring, summer and early autumn are the times to harvest and enjoy. The real work absolutely must be done in the 'invisible' months of late autumn and winter.

I accept that my livelihood does not depend on the output of my allotment, but apart from the occasional back-breaking physical task, work on the plot never feels like a chore. It is mentally liberating. I'm convinced that some of my finest inspiration has come when I've been within a stone's throw of my allotment shed. Perhaps it was a programme idea, or the decision to propose to my wife Natasha, or maybe an idea for using a glut of beetroot. For me, every turn of the soil is a step towards a fabulous future feast – the ingredients just haven't grown yet. Such optimism and fantasy are essential qualities for the veg grower.

The net result of all the physical exertion and cerebral exhilaration is an abundance of fresh seasonal produce almost all the year round, which brings me to cooking. If ever a person needs to have a 'positive relationship' with vegetables it's when they have eaten the same crop every day for a fortnight. The inconvenient truth is that unless the grower finds a new way to cook the mountain of whatever veg they see before them, it will end up as compost. When you have known each individual plant since it was a seed, that's not an easy thought. Culinary creativity is the saviour. All those days spent gazing at emerging green shoots and fantasising about the flavours now prove worthwhile. At times, recipes germinate in my head and simply need to be converted to action when a crop is harvested. At other times my culinary creations are more evolutionary, born of the necessity to magic something from the ingredients at hand, in an effort to avoid the shops.

Between plot and plate, often much changes. I have a pretty freestyle approach to cooking, so although I may have a dish in mind when the veg hit the wheelbarrow, it doesn't always materialise. The distinctive aroma that arises when cutting into a vegetable may spark an idea, though the end result will also depend on what else is in the cupboard. This is the joy of cooking. Of course improvisation can end in culinary disaster, yet I believe that true creativity comes about by accident, through instinct, experiment, passion and taste.

The recipes are seasonal by nature. My dishes tend to be heartier in the winter as a result. I prefer nourishing, slow-cooked dishes that fill the kitchen with warmth when it's cold outside, such as a winter chicken casserole laden with carrots and parsnips, or a creamy, rich beetroot risotto radiating sweetness from the pan. In summer I tend to spend less time in the kitchen and more outside. Tuna with lime and cucumber or a colourful salad ooze sunshine from the plate and are a delightful prelude to a lazy afternoon. Then when the last of the sun's rays set and the heat leaves the earth, a light courgette soup with mint and feta closes the day perfectly.

Finally, I urge you to at least try growing something from seed; nurture, cook and eat it – for no better reason than to experience one of life's most satisfying and fundamental pleasures.

The plot

I have had several allotments as my life has evolved, but my current plot is by far the best and most rewarding. The main reason is the location: it backs on to my garden. Every morning when I open the curtains, it nods back at me. Consequently the pressure to keep it in good order is as much aesthetic as an urge for good housekeeping. All my other plots have been out of sight and therefore mind. I have been less kind to them as a result and they have responded accordingly. Doing a little work on a regular basis is the most productive approach.

I have two sheds, both inherited. The previous occupant, known affectionately as 'two-sheds Sean', kept his tools in one and a chair in the other for when he needed to shelter from the weather. Sean had the plot for years and manured it, turned it and meticulously weeded it day after day for seasons. When he gave up the plot, I took it over, though I still leave one of the sheds unlocked in case he is passing.

The plot is big: I'd guess 70 metres long and nine metres wide. It has a slight slope to the west, which ensures that it catches every last ray of sun. It also means that it is well drained. The annually manured soil is dark, deep and rich.

In front of the sheds I have put up a greenhouse. In early spring it is home to pots of seedlings, but I also plant salad crops in the ground and later grow tomatoes and cucumbers as well. Around the greenhouse I have several raised beds with recycled floorboards as edging. These patches of fine crumb, well-drained soil are perfect for root veg, broad beans, spinach, chard and alliums such as onions, shallots and garlic. I have an area for shrubby herbs, another for flowers and a patch for perennials such as rhubarb, asparagus and globe artichokes.

A permanent bed of strawberries spans the width of the plot, as does an area for raspberries, currants and gooseberries. Beyond that I rotate a number of crops. Every plant takes particular nutrients from the soil and adds others. Rotating ensures that the soil recovers and the plants get what they need. It also means that diseases affecting any particular crop don't return. So I currently have a large bed for potatoes and a similar sized area for pumpkins and squash. There is a patch for brassicas (cabbages, kale, broccoli, sprouts, pak choi and so on) and space for climbing beans of many varieties – runners, French, borlottis, for example. I also have room for sweetcorn and courgettes and anything else I can pack in. At the far end are a few fruit trees beside a little pond I created for frogs in the hope they would repay me by eating all the slugs. I should have built a bigger one.

And so that's the plot: peaceful, beautiful and always generous.

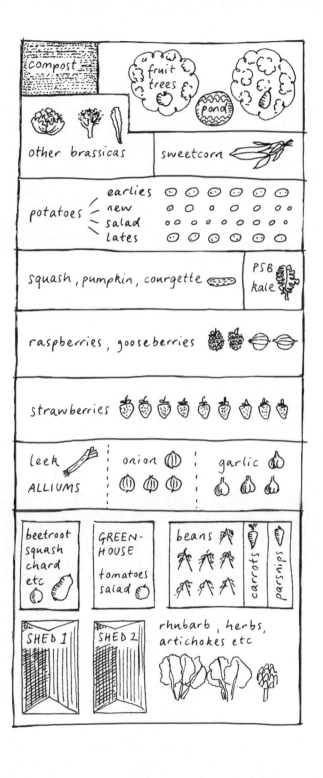

Spring

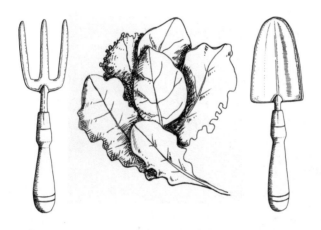

What to plant and harvest in spring

Sow

basil

climbing beans

beetroot

broccoli

cabbages

carrots

celery

chillies

coriander

courgettes

cucumbers

kale

leeks

pak choi

parsnips

peas

pumpkins

radishes

rocket

salad leaves

spinach

sprouts

squash

sweetcorn

tomatoes

Plant

Jerusalem artichokes

onion and shallot sets

potatoes

Harvest

asparagus

broccoli

broad beans

chard

chives and other herbs

nettles

pea shoots

purple sprouting broccoli

radishes

rhubarb

rocket

salad leaves

spring onions

wild garlic

SPRING RECIPES

Asparagus

Asparagus on its own
Asparagus and leek soup with wild garlic
Asparagus risotto

Broad beans

Broad bean hummus
Broad bean and mint pâté
Chorizo and broad beans
Bacon, broad bean and pea salad

Chard

Fishcakes with wilted chard
Chard, red pepper and feta frittata

Spring herbs

Herb oils
Lamb chops with garlic, thyme and parsley

Nettles and wild garlic

Nettle and wild garlic soup

Shell-on prawns with wild garlic mayonnaise

Pea shoots

*Pea shoot, watercress and avocado salad
with lemon and olive oil dressing*

Scallops with pea shoots, thyme and pancetta

Purple sprouting broccoli

Spicy pork and purple sprouting broccoli

Purple sprouting broccoli and Stilton soup

Purple sprouting broccoli and Parma ham au gratin

Radishes

'Blow your mind' salsa

Radish tzatziki

Rhubarb

Warming rhubarb and ginger crumble with custard

Panna cotta with poached rhubarb

Rocket

Rocket pesto with sirloin and red wine

Poached salmon with buttery rocket sauce

Salad leaves

Baby leaves with mustard dressing

Grilled goat's cheese salad
with roasted shallot, balsamic and walnut dressing

Spring onions

Scrambled eggs and spring onions on sourdough toast

Steamed pollack with ginger and spring onions

A change is as good as a rest.
On your marks…

By March, the allotment has endured long dark winter days, frost and quite possibly snow. Thankfully, very soon, nature suddenly decides it's time to 'spring'. After lying semi-dormant and glum for several months, I may at last wake up and blossom into action.

Waiting for nature's invitation to plant is like being a toddler waiting for Santa. I find myself almost 'counting the sleeps' until the fear of frost has disappeared. While most sane people huddle under the duvet in denial of the morning, the keen grower can't wait to venture out. On these crisp, sunny mornings, cars need scraping and schoolchildren huddle and idle with steaming breath. The hardy veg grower, though, will often be spotted in the distance, tramping over the white blanket that hugs the solid black earth. The solitary figure will occasionally kick a hefty clump and fantasise about the season ahead. It's often too cold to actually do anything, but think-ing about it is often the best bit. Very occasionally, thinking and digging are possible at the same time, in a multitasking unison of brain and brawn. Perfection.

Caution is advisable. Nature is a continually shifting beast. Spring weather varies wildly and understanding it determines success or failure. Get it wrong and you will wake one morning to find all seedlings destroyed by a late frost. Get it right and your plants will crop earlier, extending the growing season, with more produce for your efforts. It may sound a tad poetic, but if the grower is really in touch with the garden and listens to nature, then instinct dictates when the time has come to plant. With such affinity, the soil almost broadcasts 'plant me; I'm ready'. So between ordering seeds at Christmas and waiting for the last frost to thaw, the alert gardener becomes twitchy, knowing the starting pistol is imminent, yet wary of making the first move. The best way to temper your eagerness is to dig. This will give the plants the best possible start in life – weed-free, growing in fine crumbs of deep fertile soil with good drainage is the vegetable equivalent of being born with a silver spoon. All it takes is a spade and determination.

From the moment spring has sprung, nature really motors on. The birds eagerly begin to nest; the soil warms, sap rises and the garden soon explodes rapidly with life. Don't miss the signs. Garden life waits for no one. Nothing demotivates the digger more than seeing a neighbour's pots overflowing with foliage in the greenhouse, when his own are mere tubs of soil. Of course it's not a competition, as I regularly remind myself (while rushing to the potting shed). Thankfully around this time, the clocks change and the days at least give the impression of being longer; coats disappear and casual jackets emerge. Fortunately, this is not a sprint. It's a marathon. It is good to get out in front early though, so you need to put on a pair of wellies pretty sharpish. A strategy helps, too.

21 March is an important milestone. Scientists and astron- omers recognise it as the vernal equinox. I can't say I was paying much attention in the geography class the day we learned about the solar system, yet for some reason the word and date lodged in my memory. Had my school offered Latin (it wasn't that kind of school), I would have discovered that equinox translates as 'equal night', a time when day and night are of equal length. Education – or lack of it – aside, I have observed over the years that the equinox is a significant turning point. Consequently, by mid-March I like to have the potatoes

planted and the first seeds snuggled in pots of compost ready to germinate. I tend to pop two to three of the larger seeds, such as courgettes and pumpkins, into each pot. They won't all grow; just select the strongest to plant out. The tinier seeds, such as tomatoes, I scatter in a larger plastic tray of compost, again later picking out the best seedlings to transplant into bigger pots as soon as they can stand on their own two feet. If any of the seeds haven't poked their heads up by mid-April, there's still time for a second sowing, but at least (if it were a race) you are warmed up and poised for the pistol.

Seed potatoes should be put in a cool, light place for a few weeks in February to encourage the shoots to appear. This is called chitting. Plant the potatoes with shoots upwards in trenches as soon as the frosts have gone. I tend to grow earlies, maincrops, lates and salad potatoes, so planting spuds is the biggest job of the year. Onions and shallots are buried to their necks in fine soil. I tend to net them for a few weeks until they bed in, as the birds like to pull them out at random.

In the greenhouse, I plant the first salad leaves and rocket straight into the ground. Over the coming weeks, I will plant a few rows of each every ten days or so. This way I can harvest daily pickings of spinach, rocket, baby chard, lamb's lettuce, radishes, mustard and mizuna for mouthwatering fresh 'interesting' salads in a matter of weeks, right through to late October.

There's plenty of decent food to be had from the plot this time of year. Early on, the purple sprouting broccoli (delicious steamed) grows with fervour. The last of the leeks, potatoes and parsnips may look a little weary, but a bowl of steaming mash topped with a nest of shredded leek and parsnip crisped in hot oil marks another full stop. I always smile to see that as the freezer empties the allotment fills.

Then the new crops arrive at speed. For me there is a synergy between what is happening in the natural world: new life, energy, buzz and the exciting fresh palate of the season. New flavours, young plants and vibrancy define spring for me. There's also a wonderful simplicity. Freshly dug, tiny new potatoes and delicate young broad beans have such richness of flavour that they need little to accompany them.

So let battle with nature commence – my palate awaits.

Asparagus

....

I have mixed feelings about asparagus. If I were on the couch, my analyst would undoubtedly point to my working-class roots and see asparagus as a symbol of the new middle class that I physically find myself in, yet mentally resist. The therapist, I'm sure, would insist that until I accept asparagus, I will struggle to live at peace. I work through it every spring.

Of course seasonal British asparagus is quite rightly universally applauded and I do love it. Yet it is a precocious child. It's the vegetable equivalent of a tricky celebrity; it needs a lot of attention – its own bed for a start. You need to keep it completely weed-free and do not even contemplate harvesting during the first three years of its life. Weed it, water it, feed it, protect it from frost, shelter it from sun and indulge it in its own space to mature. When all the pantomime and nurturing is done, the grower must wait patiently for the crowns (not just heads), to make their theatrical entrance. Then we indulge it. Stories of eager cooks sitting by asparagus beds with a pan of boiling water are common and there are the affluent armies who insist on asparagus pans, steamers and specialist cookers. *It's only a vegetable!* Having said all this, it does have an amazing flavour. Asparagus spears are ready to pick mid-April, marking the beginning of lighter, warmer days and it is at its celebrated best for just a precious, short six weeks.

ASPARAGUS ON ITS OWN

You have to do it! Not to do it would be like refusing to join the office sweepstake for the Grand National, going to bed early on New Year's Eve, or not having a social media presence. You would definitely feel you were missing out. You might even turn into a grouch – so just do it and then it's done. If you are going to eat asparagus on its own, I recommend picking your own; there are a scattering of places around.

SERVES 2

150g asparagus, woody ends snapped off
30g salted butter
fine salt

Bring a large saucepan of water to the boil and add a generous pinch of salt. Add the asparagus and cook for 4–5 minutes or until just cooked. Never be tempted to overcook asparagus! Drain immediately and serve with a generous knob of butter.

Variation: asparagus is a perfect pairing with egg. Try dipping blanched asparagus spears into a soft-boiled egg or serve them slathered in hollandaise sauce.

ASPARAGUS AND LEEK SOUP
WITH WILD GARLIC

It may seem a little indulgent using asparagus in a soup, but there is a limit to the number of times you can eat it on its own, and the leek and wild garlic make wonderful seasonal companions in a dish that is crammed with vitality and flavour. Wild garlic, also known as ramsons, is an easy crop to grow, but you can also find it in damp woodland areas in spring. You will recognise it by the distinctive garlic smell given off by the leaves, as well as the small, starry white flowers.

SERVES 3–4

2 medium leeks,
 very finely chopped
50g unsalted butter
10ml olive oil
150g asparagus,
 chopped into rings
1 litre chicken stock

250ml double cream
6 wild garlic leaves,
 very finely chopped
flaked sea salt and
 freshly ground white pepper
crusty bread, to serve

Pop the leeks into a large saucepan with the butter and oil. Add a little salt and cook on a low heat, so as not to colour the leeks. Add the asparagus rings to the leeks as they soften. Stir and add the chicken stock. After simmering for ten minutes, remove the pan from the heat and blitz the contents with an electric hand blender. You don't have to have a silky smooth texture; a few bits are fine. Pour in the cream and return the soup to the stove to heat through for a couple of minutes.

Add the wild garlic leaves to the soup. When they have softened, ladle the soup into bowls, grind over a sprinkling of white pepper and serve with crusty bread.

ASPARAGUS RISOTTO

*Risotto is the vegetable grower's friend. As long as I have some
Arborio rice in the cupboard, a hunk of Parmesan and a few veg,
I know I will have a satisfying meal. This is the perfect comfort dish;
therapy for the taste buds. Perhaps more importantly, it is such a
relaxing dish to cook. I don't know why, but something happens when
the rice loses all its inhibitions, softens and surrenders to the liquid.
On cue my shoulders relax and I find myself being absorbed into
the cooking process, stirring the rice as the stress disappears.*

SERVES 4

1 large onion, finely chopped
50g unsalted butter
400g Arborio rice
150g asparagus,
    ends discarded,
    sliced into 1cm lengths

200ml dry white wine
1.5 litres warm chicken stock
60g Parmesan, grated,
    plus extra to serve
150ml crème fraiche

Heat the widest heavy saucepan you have and sauté the
onions in the butter. Add the rice and stir so that every grain
is coated, keeping the heat low so it doesn't burn or stick.
Put the asparagus in the saucepan, keeping the tips for later.

Pour in the white wine, stirring continuously. As the wine
is absorbed, gradually ladle in the warm stock, a splosh at a
time, stirring as you go. The amount of stock you need varies
depending on how quickly you cook, so use your judgement.
The risotto should glisten with moisture – don't let it dry out
and stick to the bottom of the saucepan. When you have used
nearly all the stock add the asparagus tips and the rest of the
liquid. Stir and cover for a few minutes.

Add the Parmesan and the crème fraiche and stir again.
The rice will be gloopy and speckled with the mushy asparagus
stems, while the tips just hold their shape. Serve in hot bowls
with a final topping of Parmesan.

Broad beans

How I hated broad beans as a child. I don't really understand why I even contemplated growing them. I think it was because they are one of the few crops that can be planted in the autumn. It was a tentative liaison at first – I was, admittedly, slightly unsure what to do with them. Now, though, as our relationship has blossomed season after season, I can proudly proclaim that I am, in fact 'in love' with broad beans. There; I've said it. They earn that right from flavour, of course, yet they also deserve respect as one of the few seeds that survive winter. Their delicate spring flowers are truly beautiful, and shortly after they bloom the first pods form. Most people encounter broad beans at the height of summer, when they are at their most robust. The furry pods are usually consigned to the compost heap and shelling the beans can feel like too much effort. I promise you that it is not. What's more, if you cultivate a few plants in pots or in a spare patch of ground, the harvesting season is much longer. The grower can feast on whole young pods in spring, or taste the sweeter young beans without having the bother of shelling them. What's not to love? Broad beans are quite happy to grow in pots if you are short of space.

BROAD BEAN HUMMUS

This stuff is pretty addictive; it's light, fresh and has an intense spring flavour.

If you catch them young enough you can use the whole pod, otherwise pod and shell the beans. Either way, 500g will make you a generous bowl of delicious dip. If the raw garlic is too much for you, try roasting the garlic first. I'd suggest using three or four cloves if you do this.

SERVES 4

500g broad beans
2 garlic cloves, peeled
1 small red chilli, deseeded, or
  1 teaspoon of chilli powder
50ml vegetable oil

2–3 tablespoons fresh
  lemon juice
50ml olive oil
1 teaspoon salt

Put the beans in a saucepan, barely cover them with salted water, then boil vigorously for about 8–10 minutes until just soft. Drain, and rinse in cold water.

Put the garlic and chilli (or chilli powder) into a food processor. Add the salt and whizz to a fine paste. Add the broad beans and two tablespoons of lemon juice and whizz again, slowly drizzling in an equal quantity of vegetable oil and olive oil. I used to stick to olive oil, but I prefer a lighter mix nowadays. To that end I also drizzle in some water to achieve the right consistency. This is a matter of personal taste: just remember that you can't thicken it if it gets too runny, so add liquid cautiously. Store the hummus in a sealed carton in the refrigerator until ready to serve. It won't keep more than a day – it's that good.

BROAD BEAN AND MINT PÂTÉ

This simple dish was an experiment and I can't tell you how excited I was when I tasted the result. Now I look forward to it every year. The pots sit in the refrigerator and are as tempting for breakfast as they are for lunch and dinner. Spread thickly on fingers of toast it is both delicate and filling. I make this recipe near the end of the season, when the beans are a little harder and the skins a tad thicker.

SERVES 6

300g podded broad beans
100g unsalted butter
15ml sherry vinegar

generous handful (about 15g) fresh mint, finely chopped
salt
buttered toast, to serve

Boil the beans in a saucepan of salted water for 10–12 minutes, then drain. Pop the flesh out of each bean and discard the skins. Melt the butter slowly in another saucepan and add the broad beans. Stir gently with a wooden spoon, and as the beans begin to turn to mush, add the sherry vinegar then the mint. When the mixture has warmed through and most of the beans have softened into the molten butter, remove the pan from the heat.

Put the contents of the saucepan into a food processor and blitz to a fairly smooth paste. You can choose whether you want a coarse, medium or fine pâté; keep back some of the bean mixture and fold it into the paste if you prefer a coarser texture. Decant into a large ramekin. Cool in the refrigerator and spread on fingers of hot buttered toast.

Variation: if the carnivores feel the need for a meaty pâté, cut some streaky bacon into very thin strips and fry over a medium–high heat until crisp in a non-stick frying pan. Don't add any fat; the bacon has its own. Fold the crisp bacon pieces into the pâté before you put it into the ramekin. Pour any leftover bacon fat over the top to seal.

CHORIZO AND BROAD BEANS

If you think you don't like broad beans, try this. Broad beans and chorizo are a spectacular combination. The chorizo has fire and energy, while the beans offer comforting flavour and texture. I use thick, fatty, spicy chorizo. This makes a good snack lunch with crusty bread, or a side. However, I predict that it will steal the show. I also guarantee that whatever quantity you cook won't be enough and that you will crave more. This was the dish I cooked with my first ever broad bean harvest and I yearn for it every year. It's soft, fragrant, buttery, spicy, creamy and indulgent.

SERVES 2

**200g podded young
  broad beans**
**150g spicy cooking chorizo,
  skinned and cubed**

200ml double cream
**bunch flat-leaf parsley
  (about 20g), finely chopped**
salt

Boil the broad beans in a saucepan of salted water for 6–7 minutes. Drain and rinse in cold water. Put the chorizo in a frying pan over a moderate heat and allow it to cook in its own fat. Remove and discard the skins from the broad beans (unless it's early in the season, when you can leave them on). Add the beans to the pan and cook through for a few minutes. As the beans start to break down and lose their shape, reduce the heat, add the cream and warm through. Sprinkle on the parsley and serve straight away.

BACON, BROAD BEAN AND PEA SALAD

Whatever the weather and wherever you tuck into this delightful salad, the joys of the season will not be far away. There is excitement in the air at this time of year. Chicks chirp in anticipation of their next feed, the flowers sway and open up to the bees and the sun's rays dance across the new leaves. This light dish encapsulates it all. Every mouthful simply tastes of spring.

SERVES 4

500g podded broad beans

200g podded peas, or
   sugar snaps, or mangetout

8 rashers fatty streaky bacon,
   cubed

4 tablespoons olive oil,
   plus extra for frying

3 thick slices slightly stale
   bread, cubed

1 tablespoon sherry vinegar

2 teaspoons finely chopped
   mint

salad leaves

30g pea shoots, to serve

In a large saucepan boil the beans and peas until soft and put to one side. (If you're using young sugar snaps or mangetout, cook them whole.) Fry the bacon in a little oil until golden. When crisp, remove from the pan and rest on kitchen paper. Fry the bread cubes in the residual bacon fat until golden. Dry on kitchen paper.

Make the dressing by combining the olive oil, the sherry vinegar and the mint in a clean, lidded jam jar and shaking it frantically. Assemble the salad (I prefer it warm, though it doesn't have to be). Drizzle over the dressing. Top with a handful of pea shoots and serve.

Chard

Chard is one perennial crop that I harvest practically all year round; the colourful stems and green leaves provide fabulous flavour. The rainbow stems don't just brighten up the allotment as they catch the sun, they do a similar job on the plate. I strip the leaves from the stalks, blanch the stems quickly in heavily salted water, then steam the torn leaves. These hold a lot of moisture, so give them a squeeze and a final chop before reuniting them with the stems in a warm bowl. I like to drizzle with a peppery olive oil, a few grinds of black pepper and a good squeeze of lemon juice. It's great as a colourful accompaniment to a pork chop alongside a few spuds.

FISHCAKES WITH WILTED CHARD

I love fishcakes. They are, more often than not, knocked together when there's some leftover fish and mash in the fridge, with other ingredients added depending on what else is about. For me though, fishcakes are so good, it's worth making a special trip to buy the ingredients – you can always freeze any extras if you make a batch. I like a high ratio of fish to potato to keep them lighter and meatier, although too little mash will give you a mush in the pan. However they come to the table, wilted chard is a delicious partner and worth making the fishcakes for.

SERVES 4–6

for the fishcakes
150g salmon fillet
**100g hake fillet
(or other firm white fish)**
sprig thyme
squeeze fresh lemon juice
2 eggs, beaten
300g mashed potato
4 spring onions, finely chopped
**bunch flat-leaf parsley
(about 20g), finely chopped**
30g capers, finely chopped
4 anchovies, finely chopped
100g smoked haddock fillet
plain flour, for dusting
100g white breadcrumbs
oil, for frying
salt and pepper

for the chard
**300g chard, washed,
stems trimmed**
knob unsalted butter
**1 clove garlic,
crushed to a paste**
**1 teaspoon finely chopped
unwaxed lemon zest**
**1 teaspoon finely chopped
coriander**
10ml chilli oil
salt

Put the salmon and hake into a saucepan with a little water, the thyme sprig and a squeeze of lemon juice. Cover and simmer for 6–7 minutes.

In a large bowl stir just over half the eggs into the mashed potato. Add the spring onions, parsley, capers and anchovies and stir. When the salmon and hake are cooked, remove from the saucepan with a slotted spoon and flake the flesh into the bowl together with the smoked haddock and a pinch of salt and pepper. Try to keep the flakes as good-sized chunks so they don't lose their texture. Shape the fishcakes into even-sized patties. Dip each in the flour, the remaining egg and the breadcrumbs. Put in the refrigerator for half an hour.

Cook the fishcakes for no more than five minutes on each side in a frying pan of hot oil. The breadcrumbs should be golden and crisp and the centre of the fishcake warmed through.

While the fishcakes are cooking put the chard in a large saucepan with a sprinkle of salt and a knob of butter. Cover the pan and cook over a high heat. After a couple of minutes the chard will wilt. Turn off the heat, drain off the liquid and cover. Stir in the garlic, lemon zest and coriander. Drizzle with chilli oil before serving.

Variation: if you have time to make one, a hollandaise sauce (see page 102) makes a lovely topping.

CHARD, RED PEPPER AND FETA FRITTATA

As the year progresses, chard grows bigger, tougher and more robust. I like to make this frittata in spring when the leaves are young and tender. It has a bit more personality than spinach and stands up well to the pepper and feta.

SERVES 4

20g unsalted butter
30g baby chard, washed
4 medium eggs, beaten
1 small red pepper, diced

10ml olive oil
75g feta
salt

Preheat the oven to 220°C/200°C fan/425°F/Gas mark 7. Melt the butter in a small saucepan and add the chard with a good pinch of salt. Cover and wilt for around five minutes. Drain and squeeze the moisture from the leaves before chopping them roughly and mixing with the eggs. Soften the pepper olive oil in a non-stick ovenproof frying pan. Reduce the heat and add the egg and chard, ensuring a good mix through the pan. Once the base starts to set, crumble over the feta and transfer the frying pan to the oven for about eight minutes, or until the egg has set. Allow to cool for a few minutes, then turn out on to a serving plate. A wedge served with salad is delicious.

Variation: Stilton also works in place of the feta and spinach can be substituted for chard.

Spring herbs

Herbs are probably the first edible plants I tended and they are both essential and lovely. Some come and go; others, if you treat them well, will stay with you for much of the year. Many develop into lifelong companions. Herbs are fantastic in pots, which allow you to rotate them, so you always have the most vibrant and healthy plants to hand. It's a good idea to have two or three pots of each herb. I also like planting out herbs so they become more shrub-like over time. I have a large, gnarled and woody rosemary that has established itself so firmly it withstands any amount of hacking. I also have an enormous bay and several varieties of thyme. Growing big herb plants means that you have huge quantities to cook with, with no fear of killing the plant.

For me the secret is not using complicated combinations of herbs. Be confident when using them. I have also realised that I prefer certain herbs at particular times of the year – I tend to use more thyme and sage in spring; tarragon, lovage, mint and basil in summer, and rosemary in the darker months.

In general, I am not a lover of supermarket pots of herbs. I much prefer to buy plants with healthy roots from a nursery, which will populate a pot or plot for a season at least. My one exception is basil. I find it pretty temperamental and slow to grow from seed. Often it's midsummer before I succeed and I can't wait that long. My friend Paul gave me a simple tip that has transformed my basil growing. Every spring, buy a supermarket pot of basil and divide the young plants between four larger pots. Put three pots in the greenhouse and one in the kitchen. Water them well, rotate them once a week and you will have a good supply of basil for months.

HERB OILS

There is great vigour in the garden in spring: young herbs with green shoots are full of aromatic oil and it would be a crime not to capture some of that magic. Herb oils look lovely on a kitchen shelf and within just a few days the natural plant oils infuse the olive oil to create wonderful subtle flavours. These oils can invigorate salads or be drizzled on soups. Empty wine bottles are ideal containers, but you can buy beautiful smaller empty bottles too. Whichever bottles you choose, make sure they are sterile by washing them in hot, soapy water, rinsing thoroughly, then drying them in a low oven before use. For the recipe below you will need two ½ litre bottles. In mid-spring I make rosemary oil and thyme oil. Both benefit from the addition of a clove of garlic and some citrus zest.

MAKES 1 LITRE

few sprigs rosemary and thyme, washed
2 cloves garlic, peeled
few strands unwaxed orange zest

1 litre peppery extra-virgin olive oil (ideally young, recently pressed)
few strands unwaxed lemon zest

Preheat the oven to its lowest setting. Lay the herbs on a baking tray in the oven. Only leave the herbs in the oven for five minutes; the idea is to ensure that they are throroughly dry, not to cook them. The warmth also helps to activate the natural oils in the herbs. Poke a few sprigs of rosemary, a garlic clove and the strands of orange zest into a bottle, then fill it with half the extra-virgin olive oil. In the other bottle pack in some thyme sprigs, a garlic clove and a few strands of lemon zest and fill it with the remaining olive oil. Seal tightly. Store in a cool place. After a week the oils will be ready to use.

LAMB CHOPS WITH GARLIC, THYME AND PARSLEY

Serving this dish on a drizzly spring day is one of my favourite treats. They may be small, but lamb chops pack so much flavour. Thyme accentuates the sweetness of the meat, and garlic and parsley complement each other well. Three chops per person look good arranged on the plate, and will provide plenty of meat.

SERVES 4

4 cloves garlic, peeled
Handful (about 15g) thyme leaves
10ml olive oil
12 lamb chops
20g unsalted butter
2 tablespoons plain flour, to dust
juice 1 lemon
300ml chicken stock
15g flat-leaf parsley, finely chopped
salt
pea shoot, watercress and avocado salad (see page 38), to serve

Preheat the oven to its lowest setting. Crush the garlic and thyme leaves in a pestle and mortar with a little salt and the olive oil, until you have a smooth paste. Pour this over the lamb chops, coating both sides. Let them sit in the mix for ten minutes or so. Drain the excess oil into a frying pan, add the butter and melt it over a medium heat. When the butter bubbles, coat each chop in flour and pop into the pan. Brown the chops for about four minutes on each side, remove and put in the warm oven.

Add the lemon juice to the frying pan and stir quickly to release the caramelised flour on the bottom, before incorporating the stock and any leftover garlic and thyme paste. Simmer for five minutes, strain, then pour over the warm lamb chops to serve. Sprinkle the flat-leaf parsley over the chops and serve with a pea shoot, watercress and avocado salad.

Nettles and wild garlic

....

Our ancestors foraged to survive, so I'm not sure why foraging feels quite so illicit today. There are probably laws that we shouldn't contravene. I do have one word of warning: be careful where you pick. I pick wild garlic and nettles in places where few dogs are walked. I also offer a piece of advice to help you avoid being stung. Nettle stems have tiny, fine hairs that point upwards and sting. My tip is to pick upwards: carefully bring your thumb and forefinger from underneath and use an upward motion as you squeeze them together to pick the nettle.

NETTLE AND WILD GARLIC SOUP

You will need roughly 1¾ carrier bags of nettles to ¼ bag of garlic leaves. Don't pick nettles with thick woody stems; go for the succulent green stems and only the top third of the plant. This is a dish for early in the season, as nettles get tougher as spring passes – better served in May than June. I also recommend giving the leaves a thorough wash.

SERVES 4

50g butter
1 tablespoon vegetable oil
1 large onion, chopped
1.75kg tender nettles, washed and roughly chopped
250g wild garlic leaves, washed and roughly chopped

300ml white wine
1.5 litres chicken stock
300ml double cream
salt and freshly ground white pepper
custy bread, to serve

Heat the butter and oil in a large saucepan over a low heat and add the onion. Cook for five minutes until softened. Add the nettles and garlic leaves to the pan, sprinkle with salt and pour in the wine. Cover the saucepan until the leaves wilt in the steam, then add the stock. Simmer for about ten minutes. Whizz with a hand blender and pour in the cream, then add a grind of white pepper. Warm through and serve with crusty bread.

SHELL-ON PRAWNS
WITH WILD GARLIC MAYONNAISE

*This is a finger-licking lunch with a sense of occasion. Shelling prawns
may be fiddly and time-consuming, but every mouthful is savoured
and cherished. There are plenty of variations of garlic mayonnaise,
but wild garlic feels right with prawns. I use a light olive oil as five egg
yolks make this mayonnaise very rich. You will have five egg whites
left over, with which you could make a pavlova, to avoid food waste.
They can also be frozen and will keep for up to a year.*

SERVES 2

5 egg yolks
1 tablespoon Dijon mustard
200ml olive oil
3 tablespoons lemon juice

**6 wild garlic leaves, washed
and very finely chopped**
250g cooked prawns, shells on
salt

Put the egg yolks, mustard and a generous pinch of salt
into a bowl and whisk vigorously. After a few minutes, very
slowly drizzle in the olive oil and lemon juice. Keep whisking.
The yolks will get lighter in colour and you will end up
with a deliciously rich mayonnaise. Add the wild garlic
and gently stir. Serve with the prawns, a beer, a newspaper
and some sunshine.

Variation: in the absence of wild garlic, use roast garlic.
I put a few bulbs of garlic in the oven when I roast potatoes,
so often have it in the refrigerator – it's milder than raw garlic.
Use the blade of a large, flexible knife and some salt to turn
five roasted garlic cloves into a paste.

Pea shoots

....

'Where have all the pea pods gone?' There's definitely a lament in there somewhere. I have to admit that I have joined the trend of using pea shoots as a tasty and decorative garnish to many a dish. They are the modern day equivalent of curly parsley, though somewhat easier to chew. This creates a dilemma on the allotment, though. I love the intensity of flavour provided by pea shoots, but routinely snipping them off so early in their lives has meant that I harvest significantly fewer peas. That said, the shoots are extremely delicious, so I just have to plant more.

PEA SHOOT, WATERCRESS AND AVOCADO SALAD WITH LEMON AND OLIVE OIL DRESSING

Pea shoots have a delicate flavour, so it's a sin to smother them in an overpowering dressing. Sometimes simplicity is king: I recommend using the best olive oil you can afford for this and chopping the parsley as finely as you are able.

SERVES 2

1 ripe avocado, peeled
50g pea shoots
50g watercress

for the dressing
150ml extra-virgin olive oil
juice 1 lemon,
 plus a few strands zest
handful flat-leaf parsley,
 finely chopped
salt and pepper

Quarter the avocado, but don't cut through the end, so you can remove the stone and slice it thinly, fanning it out on a plate. Scatter over handfuls of pea shoots and watercress. To make the dressing, put all the ingredients into a clean, lidded jam jar, screw on the lid and shake it vigorously, then drizzle the dressing sparsely on the leaves.

Variation: this dressing is also lovely on freshly dug new potatoes or grilled slices of aubergine.

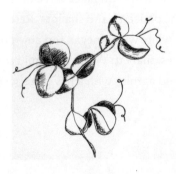

SCALLOPS WITH PEA SHOOTS, THYME AND PANCETTA

On spring days when the sun breaks through the morning haze and you need to find your sunglasses, a quick, luxurious al fresco lunch with a chilled rosé is a simple yet celebratory pleasure. Scallops are expensive, but you only need a few to make a bold statement. Coupled with salty, crisp pancetta and garnished with pea shoots and thyme, this dish will bring elegance to your afternoon.

SERVES 2

sprig thyme, leaves finely chopped

30g pea shoots, finely chopped, plus a few to garnish

50g pancetta, cubed

2 small shallots, finely chopped

30ml olive oil

6 scallops

20ml white wine vinegar

freshly ground black pepper

Put the chopped thyme leaves and pea shoots on a small saucer. Heat your heaviest frying pan over a high heat. When very hot add the pancetta cubes. After a couple of minutes, when they start to crisp, lower the heat. Add the shallots and stir until they are translucent.

In a separate frying pan heat the olive oil until hot and sear the scallops for no longer than a minute on each side. Season with a grind of pepper, then coat each scallop in the chopped pea shoots and thyme and place three on each serving plate. Spoon over the pancetta and shallots. Return the pan to the heat, add the white wine vinegar and any remaining chopped leaves to the residual fat. Warm the liquid through, pour over the scallops and garnish with a few pea shoots.

Purple sprouting broccoli

Purple sprouting broccoli symbolises the circle of life: when each plant is in its prime and I am harvesting tender spears on a daily basis, I have already planted the following year's seeds. The mature plants are big, strong and productive. The seeds, by contrast, appear tiny and vulnerable. Yet in just a few short weeks, their fortunes are reversed. Just when I think that I can't eat any more purple sprouting broccoli, the small violet sprouts start to bloom into beautiful yellow flowers. For twelve months I have raised and nurtured these magnificent giants, and now they have served their purpose their final journey is to the compost heap. Meanwhile the tiny seeds I planted a few weeks ago are starting their journey. From 20 or so seeds, I often end up with five fully grown plants. In adulthood they are prolific and I never go short of purple sprouting. The purple spears and deep green leaves have incredible flavour and I can't imagine a spring without it.

SPICY PORK AND PURPLE SPROUTING BROCCOLI

Purple sprouting broccoli mingles wonderfully with pork. This is true of any brassica, but broccoli's slight bitterness complements the sweetness of the pork particularly well in this spicy dish. Pork tenderloin is excellent for a stir-fry; it's very lean and meaty, but you need to cook it quickly so it doesn't dry out. For that reason, it's worth preparing all the ingredients before you start. I like to eat this with udon noodles. The sticky sauce seeps into the noodles and it tastes sublime.

SERVES 4

2 teaspoons coriander seeds

2 teaspoons fennel seeds

400g pork tenderloin fillet, cut into bite-sized pieces

30ml coconut oil

2cm piece ginger, peeled and finely chopped

3 medium-sized red chillis, deseeded and finely chopped

2 stalks lemongrass, bruised and finely chopped

2 tablespoons clear honey

1 large leek, cut into 5cm pieces

3 Kaffir lime leaves

5 cloves garlic, peeled and quartered

200g purple sprouting broccoli, cut into 5cm pieces

1 tablespoon soy sauce

2 tablespoons sesame seeds

75g crushed peanuts

juice and zest of 1 lime

salt

Grind the coriander and fennel seeds in a pestle and mortar. Mix them with the pork pieces and leave for about ten minutes.

Heat the coconut oil in a frying pan or wok until almost spitting. Add the pork, coriander and fennel seeds and remove from the heat. Sprinkle with salt, add the ginger, chillis and lemongrass and keep stirring until the pork is coated in the spices and caramelised on the outside. Working quickly, drizzle in the honey, add the leek, lime leaves, garlic and broccoli and return the pan to a low heat.

After a couple of minutes, add the soy sauce and lime juice.

Increase the heat while the pork absorbs the liquid and the broccoli softens. Serve while there is still some texture in the leek and broccoli pieces, garnished with a scattering of sesame seeds, crushed peanuts and lime zest.

PURPLE SPROUTING BROCCOLI AND STILTON SOUP

This is a strong tasting soup. The broccoli stands up well against the Stilton. It is rich and indulgent and will fill you up, yet leave the taste buds yearning for more. I usually make it when the plants are close to their end and strip every last possible stalk.

SERVES 4

10ml vegetable oil
250g purple sprouting broccoli, stems finely chopped, heads roughly chopped
1 medium potato, peeled and cubed
1 large leek, chopped

2 sticks celery, chopped
1.5 litres chicken stock
75g Stilton
salt and freshly ground black pepper
crusty bread, to serve

Pour the oil into a large saucepan over a gentle heat and add the broccoli stems, potato, leek and celery. Sprinkle with salt, cover and allow to sweat for about five minutes.

Add the stock and increase the heat to a simmer for a further ten minutes. Blitz the soup in a blender and then return to the pan over a low heat. Crumble in most of the Stilton and add the broccoli heads. Stir occasionally for around five minutes over a low heat, so the Stilton melts and the broccoli heads cook through. Serve with a few more crumbs of Stilton, a grind of pepper and crusty bread.

PURPLE SPROUTING BROCCOLI AND PARMA HAM AU GRATIN

The combination of salty Parma ham and robust broccoli smothered in a creamy, cheesy sauce results in a delicious family lunch. This will even entice the most reluctant toddler to eat broccoli. Serve with boiled new potatoes and butter.

SERVES 4

40g unsalted butter
40g plain flour
500ml milk
75g Gruyère, grated
1 tablespoon Worcestershire sauce

1 tablespoon Dijon mustard
200ml crème fraiche
300g purple sprouting broccoli spears
8 slices Parma ham

Preheat the oven to 190°C/170°C fan/375°F/Gas mark 5. Make a roux by gently melting the butter in a saucepan and stirring in the flour to form a paste. It will take a couple of minutes to cook through. Take the pan from the heat and slowly stir in the milk, using a balloon whisk to avoid lumps. Return to a gentle heat and simmer. Add most of the Gruyère and allow it to melt into the sauce. Keep stirring. When the cheese has completely melted, turn off the heat and stir in the Worcestershire sauce, mustard and crème fraiche.

Wrap four or five broccoli spears in each slice of Parma ham and lay them in a buttered ovenproof dish. Pour over the cheese sauce and bake in the oven for 30 minutes. Before serving, scatter the remaining cheese over the top and flash under the grill to bubble and brown.

Radishes

Radishes remind me of my dad. After returning from Burma in the Second World War, my father found work as a waiter. By the time I was born in the mid-sixties, he had waited tables on the Royal Train, at Kensington Palace, the Dorchester and a string of other top hotels, and had reached the prestigious position of head waiter at the Savoy. This was a glamorous world for him to gaze into, yet inevitably he worked long hours for modest pay.

By the late seventies, we had moved from London to a council house in Devon. We had a postage stamp sized garden, yet under the shadow of the whirly washing line, Dad persevered with a few rows of radishes and parsley. On Wednesday evenings, when my mum went out, he would let me machine roll his weekly ration of cigarettes, choose a row of 'x's for the football pools and share his crisp red radishes dipped in salt. When he died, Dad didn't leave me money, but I did inherit a great set of old restaurant menus and some keen taste buds. You can't put a value on that. I'm sure he would be happy that every time I pull a radish from the ground, I think of him.

Radishes grow from seed to maturity in around five weeks and take up very little space. I grow a lot of varieties, including pink French breakfast, crimson Cherry Belles, yellow Ravanello Zlata, white Japanese mooli and dark Spanish Nero Tondo. They range in flavour from mild to incredibly hot. I love their crisp texture. When you grow the odd row here or there, as I do, you need to harvest them pretty regularly. If you don't, they will quickly go to seed and taste woody, so the trick is to eat little and often. Every Wednesday with a glass of cider is not a bad idea.

'BLOW YOUR MIND' SALSA

Some chefs talk about food marriages and relationships when referring to ingredients. This dish brings together a couple of fast-growing, small, yet powerful ingredients: radishes and rocket. On their own they can be eye-wateringly good; together they create an explosion of heat. I'd go so far as to say that they are almost too feisty to handle, undoubtedly hot-headed and need to be tamed. So, I team them up with a couple of chilled, slow growing and reassuring fellows – cucumber and mint. Thick-skinned cucumbers mature slowly over time and mint is a constant presence in the herb bed. Together they temper the fiery younger ingredients and bring calm to the palate. The ingredients for this salsa could be grown in a few pots on a windowsill. It's a show-stopping side to a meaty burger: the vigour of youth tempered by mellow maturity in each mouthful.

SERVES 4

150g radishes, chopped into bite-sized cubes

150g cucumber, chopped into bite-sized cubes

150g peppery rocket or wild rocket leaves, torn

handful mint leaves, torn

juice 1 lime

4 tablespoons extra-virgin olive oil

2 pinches sea salt

Sprinkle the radish and cucumber cubes with sea salt. Combine the rocket and mint leaves and add the lime juice and oil before mixing with the radish and cucumber.

Variation: a few finely chopped spring onions can enhance this dish.

RADISH TZATZIKI

I first tasted this dish in a small tavern in northern Kefalonia. Under the shade of a huge olive tree, the midday mezze just kept coming: dish after dish of delightful food. We hadn't actually ordered much; I think they knew that every plateful would be too tempting to turn away. A great deal of red wine accompanied each mouthful, and my Greek is limited at the best of times, so although I asked for the recipe for this mouthwatering pink starter, all I remember hearing from the chef was grated radish; the rest is a delightful blur. Grating the radishes is quite tricky; I have tried doing it in a food processor, but have also had success using a fine cheese grater. Quantity of garlic is really a personal choice: sitting in the Greek sunshine contemplating a long siesta, too much garlic doesn't seem a problem, but if you're considering taking the leftover dip to work for lunch, perhaps a little less might be appropriate. Four medium cloves for two big bunches of radishes is enough to give a good kick, without overpowering the radishes or your work colleagues.

SERVES 2

250g radishes, grated
4 cloves garlic, finely chopped
1 teaspoon paprika,
  plus extra to garnish
1 tablespoon fresh lemon juice

100g Greek yoghurt
chopped chives
salt
crusty bread, to serve

Mix the grated radishes and chopped garlic together in a small bowl. Sprinkle over a little salt, the paprika and then the lemon juice. Give it a quick mix, then put it in the refrigerator for about 20 minutes to marinate, stirring occasionally.

When you are ready to eat, pour off any excess liquid. The mixture doesn't need to be squeezed dry, just not swimming in liquid. Spoon over the Greek yoghurt and stir. A sprinkling of paprika and a scattering of chopped chives finish the dish. Serve with crusty bread and red wine.

Rhubarb

....

A plot without rhubarb is like a child without a bicycle. Rhubarb is the grower's reliable friend: it never lets you down and comes back year after year, quietly growing in the corner, waiting to be remembered. In return the grower occasionally puts some manure on it. That's friendship.

I have a few crowns of rhubarb and I usually put an upturned bucket over a couple of them in late winter – forcing them to get a move on. The resulting lanky rhubarb is more delicate than the slower growing summer stems, but still packed full of flavour. Being such a faithful provider, the more you pick, the more rhubarb grows – let's get ready to crumble.

WARMING RHUBARB AND GINGER CRUMBLE WITH CUSTARD

This is one of my favourite puds. The combination of the sweet, buttery, indulgent topping and the sharp rhubarb with warming ginger is heavenly. Adding oats to the crumble is optional and controversial. The purists wouldn't dream of it, but I think they add interest. If you would rather stick to convention, substitute with flour. Smothered in hot, thick, creamy custard, this dish has Sunday afternoon written all over it. Eaten cold with a dollop of yoghurt on a Monday evening it's pretty delicious too. You won't reach Tuesday with any leftovers...

SERVES 4–6

700g rhubarb,
  cut in 2½cm lengths
1–2 tablespoons caster sugar
25g unsalted butter, cubed
3 teaspoons dried ginger

for the crumble topping
250g cold unsalted butter,
  cubed
175g caster sugar
150g rolled oats
275g plain flour

for the custard
4 medium eggs, yolks only
30g caster sugar
2 teaspoons cornflour
500ml full fat milk
1 vanilla pod

Lightly butter an ovenproof dish and preheat the oven to 220°C/200°C fan/425°F/Gas mark 7. Arrange the rhubarb lengths in the bottom of the dish. Sprinkle with the sugar, dot with the butter and sprinkle with the ginger.

To make the crumble, rub together the butter, sugar, oats and flour until the mixture has the consistency of coarse breadcrumbs. It doesn't have to be an even mix – a few lumps are fine. (If that alarms you, give it a quick blitz in the blender, but add the oats, whole, at the end.) Gently spoon the mixture onto the rhubarb and bake in the oven for 40 minutes. As it cooks, the rhubarb juices will mix with the butter and bubble through the topping. Leave the crumble to stand for ten minutes before serving.

To make the custard, whisk the egg yolks in a bowl with the caster sugar, using a balloon whisk. The mixture will lighten and the grains from the sugar will disappear. When you have a light, smooth mixture, add the cornflour and whisk again. In a saucepan gently heat the milk. Scrape in the seeds from the vanilla pod and put the whole pod in too, for good measure. (If you are feeling indulgent you can replace up to half of the milk with double cream.) When the milk is just beneath a simmer, fish out the vanilla pod and then gently and slowly pour the milk into the egg mixture, whisking continuously.

When you have whisked in all the milk and the mixture is velvety smooth, pour it into a clean pan. Gently heat the custard, stirring regularly. Don't let it catch on the bottom of the pan; the intention is to warm it through and allow it to thicken a little – five minutes is perfect. The longer you heat it, the thicker it will get.

Variation: if you are not keen on ginger or find it too spicy, try using a couple of teaspoons of freshly chopped lovage. It's a great herb and adds a warm flavour to the pudding.

PANNA COTTA WITH POACHED RHUBARB

*I adore the decadence of panna cotta. It's delicious on its own, yet the
addition of fruit increases its luxuriousness. Rhubarb is probably my
favourite addition, especially in the spring when the forced stems are
thin and delicate, rather than later in the season when the stems are
thicker and I prefer to add soft berries. Forced early rhubarb does tend
to be thin and gangly; try to cut stems of roughly equal length for the
best looking version of this dish. Pieces about eight centimetres long
fit perfectly in my saucepan and on my favourite serving plates.*

SERVES 4 (125ml portions)

for the panna cotta
250ml double cream
300ml full fat milk
1 vanilla pod
50g caster sugar
3 sheets gelatine
vegetable oil for greasing

for the poached fruit
200g rhubarb,
    cut in 8cm pieces
30g caster sugar
300ml water
1 teaspoon cinnamon
2 cloves
2 peppercorns

Place your ramekins or moulds in the freezer before you start.
To make the panna cotta, gently warm the cream and milk in
a saucepan. Add the seeds from the vanilla pod and the empty
pod, as well as the sugar. When the sugar has dissolved and
the cream is just below a simmer (no hotter), remove the pan
from the heat and discard the vanilla pod. Soak the gelatine
leaves in cold water for five minutes until soft, and then stir
into the milky liquid. When they have completely dissolved,
remove the ramekins from the freezer, make sure they are dry
and wipe the insides with a dribble of vegetable oil on a piece
of kitchen paper. Pour the mixture into the moulds. Give
them a little tap to free any air bubbles and place on a tray
in the refrigerator.

For the poached fruit, lay the rhubarb pieces in a saucepan with the caster sugar and the water. Ideally, the water should come about a third of the way up the rhubarb, so adjust the quantity of water accordingly. Add the cinnamon, cloves and peppercorns. Poach for about four minutes. The rhubarb should be soft, yet firm enough not to disintegrate. The timing is critical as it's easy to overcook the fruit. Remove the rhubarb and put it on a plate in the refrigerator to cool. Sieve the remaining liquid and reduce it to a syrup in a saucepan over a high heat. Cool in the refrigerator.

To serve, turn the panna cotta onto one side of a plate. Neatly lay a row of four pieces of rhubarb on the other side, and then another row on top of that, facing the other way. Drizzle over the syrup, hot or cold, and serve. The rhubarb will be tart, the panna cotta light and sweet, while the cinnamon, clove and pepper undertones of the syrup pull all the flavours together.

Rocket

....

There's obviously a clue in the name, but boy does rocket grow fast. It's one of the first spring crops and if you plant successively every couple of weeks, you will have a daily helping of rocket from April right through to late October – or even November in a greenhouse. Rocket possesses a deep and powerful flavour. It is the immature and irreverent upstart of the patch and there is nothing delicate or modest about its presence. It's a grown-up taste and its power should never be underestimated. I grow two sorts of rocket: a standard broad-leaved variety and wild rocket, which has finer leaves and tends to self seed all over the place.

I have much to thank the mighty rocket for; in short it helped me when I proposed to my wife Natasha. I contemplated proposing for a long time, and came to the conclusion that it would be a very good idea indeed. It was the next stage that involved the sleepless nights and anxiety attacks. Knowing that the inevitable 'how did he propose?' questions from friends and acquaintances would follow a positive response to my question, I went into panic mode. Around that time, quite a few friends had got engaged. They had been asked in hot air balloons, up the Eiffel Tower, overlooking a Maldivian sunset, in a cave and so on. My default romantic solution of proposing by a log fire and over a delicious meal just didn't feel exciting enough. I realised (whilst turning over a clump of earth, in fact) that the only thing preventing me from popping the question was the mode of delivery. Rocket came to my rescue. Five weeks later, on a warm, sunny spring day, I took the love of my life to the allotment. There, despite an initial protest (because it was quite muddy), she lifted back a plastic cloche and was presented with a row of rapidly grown rocket spelling out the question. It blew her mind (it was a lot of rocket). Of course the romantic meal followed and there were no surprises as to what was on the menu. Later that evening as our wine glasses chinked, she confided that she had been anticipating a large rock, rather than a rocket salad.

ROCKET PESTO WITH SIRLOIN
AND RED WINE

This dish was inspired by a Tuscan holiday in a villa outside a small village, about 30 kilometres from Siena. On the first night, we followed the locals into what turned out to be a musical show by a touring choir. I've never particularly loved opera, yet when the female vocalist started to belt out Puccini's 'O mio babbino caro' I was blown away. Afterwards, we retired to the only restaurant. My main course was tagliata: rare sirloin, thinly sliced, on a bed of rocket, with Parmesan shavings. It was served on a wooden board with the juices from the pan, lemon juice, garlic and olive oil drizzled over the top and accompanied by a carafe of red wine. This simple dish oozed flavour: the saltiness of the Parmesan and the peppery rocket were perfect savoury accompaniments to the juicy steak. Like the performance that preceded it, the dish was confident, authentic, spectacular, yet understated. This dish encompasses all my memories of that evening. Don't fret about making a side dish of fries, or roasted onions or a salad or bread. Be confident and enjoy it for what it is: sensational.

SERVES 2

3 medium cloves garlic, peeled
200g rocket leaves
20ml freshly squeezed
  lemon juice
100ml extra-virgin olive oil
60g Parmesan, finely grated

olive oil, for frying
2 × 500g thick cut sirloin
  steaks
splash red wine vinegar
flaked sea salt

Pound the garlic cloves to a paste in a large pestle and mortar with a pinch of salt. Add the rocket and lemon juice. Pound again as you slowly pour in the olive oil. Finally, combine with the Parmesan and give it one final mix: it will be an amazing vibrant green. Chill in the refrigerator.

Put a heavy frying pan over a high heat and when it's hot, cook the steaks in just a little oil for about three minutes on each side. Ideally the outside will caramelise and the middle will remain juicy and red – it's essential that the steaks are rare. Remove the steaks and set them to one side to rest. Pour off any excess oil and deglaze the pan with a splash of red wine vinegar and a little water.

Slice the steaks into 2cm strips, place them in the centre of the plates and drizzle over the juices from the pan. Pour over a generous stream of pesto. Pour the wine, turn up the Puccini and eat immediately.

Variation: the pesto is also great with pasta, and delicious on roast chicken, too.

POACHED SALMON
WITH BUTTERY ROCKET SAUCE

A thick, rich, buttery sauce is the perfect traditional accompaniment to poached salmon. The rocket cuts through the richness just enough to add freshness without overpowering the other flavours. The combination is spectacular.

SERVES 2

for the sauce
4 large shallots, finely chopped
**150ml dry white wine,
   such as Chardonnay**
60ml white wine vinegar
**120g cold unsalted butter,
   cubed**
75g rocket leaves

for the salmon
**2 salmon fillets,
   about 200g each**
200ml white wine
100ml water
**1 teaspoon whole
   black peppercorns**

To make the sauce, put the shallots in a saucepan with the white wine and the wine vinegar. Heat slowly for about ten minutes. The liquid will reduce considerably. Gradually add the cold butter cubes, whisking as you go. Don't let the pan get too hot. Once you have a velvety rich sauce, remove the pan from the heat. Keep it warm and whisk the sauce from time to time while you cook the fish.

Put the salmon fillets in a large saucepan. Add the peppercorns, white wine and water. Cover with a lid and heat to a simmer for 6–7 minutes. Don't be tempted to leave it longer, or it will overcook.

Meanwhile, chop about a third of the rocket very finely and stir gently into the butter sauce. Serve the salmon on the remaining rocket, covered with a blanket of the buttery rocket sauce.

Salad leaves

When the first salads are ready, it's like New Year for the veg grower. I plant salad in the greenhouse as early as March and it's astounding how quickly it turns from a few green pinheads into a real crop. At first the tiny green specks are almost invisible; so sparse they could be weeds. Slowly little rows appear and you realise that they aren't weeds after all. Even then it's hard to imagine that these tiny plants will soon be so abundant that you'll struggle to eat them fast enough. The daily crop of vibrant, delicate, green leaves carefully snipped from the ground really does feel like a fresh start – invigorating, even. For a brief moment the thought of taking up jogging, giving up alcohol and having yoghurt for breakfast seems acceptable. Of course such crazy resolutions are fleeting – I call them my Salad Daze. Meanwhile, the leaves just keep on growing.

My childhood recollections define the lettuce of the seventies and early eighties as bitter, beige and lethargic, but things have changed. Today salads seem much more interesting and they appear in glorious vibrant colours.

BABY LEAVES WITH MUSTARD DRESSING

The variety of leaves makes each mouthful of spring salad an adventure. I combine the delicate, subtle flavours of round leaf, salad bowl and oak leaf lettuce with the more distinctive tastes of mizuna, mustard leaves, rocket, spinach and lamb's lettuce. Often there's some baby chard, sorrel and the odd dandelion leaf too. The dressing is as simple as it gets and ties everything together. I vary the quantities occasionally depending on how viscous I want the dressing to be. A good guide is to use three parts oil to one part vinegar (or lemon juice). The overall experience is enough to make you give up meat for good, grow a beard and wear sandals with white socks. I guess it shows just how far we have come since the seventies.

SERVES 2

for the salad

a selection of washed baby salad leaves:
   round leaf lettuce,
   salad bowl lettuce,
   oak leaf lettuce, mizuna,
   mustard leaves, rocket,
   baby spinach or chard,
   lamb's lettuce, sorrel,
   dandelion

for the dressing

2 tablespoons Dijon mustard
50ml white wine vinegar or lemon juice
150ml olive oil
pinch salt

Arrange the leaves on a plate. Put all the dressing ingredients in a clean, screw-topped jar and shake vigorously until combined. Pour over the leaves.

Variation: this dressing is also delicious drizzled over a thick slice of ham.

GRILLED GOAT'S CHEESE SALAD WITH ROASTED SHALLOT, BALSAMIC AND WALNUT DRESSING

A delicate mix of peppery salad leaves makes this dish an ideal spring lunch, perfect with a crisp white wine. The dressing is best made well in advance and poured at the last minute, drizzled over the salad from a height at the table. The salad leaves balance its richness and the goat's cheese and walnuts make this a substantial and delightful meal.

SERVES 4

8 shallots, peeled
60ml extra-virgin olive oil, plus extra to cook the shallots
20ml balsamic vinegar, plus extra to cook the shallots

240g soft rind goat's cheese (60g per person), sliced
40g walnuts, roughly chopped
200g mixed salad leaves
salt

Preheat the oven to 190°C/170°C fan/375°F/Gas mark 5. Put the shallots in a small ovenproof dish. Coat in a little oil and a few drops of balsamic vinegar and sprinkle with salt. Place in the oven and cook for about 30 minutes. The trick is to let the shallots soften, rather than colour too much. Long slow cooking is the best approach.

When the shallots are squidgy and sweet, blitz with a hand whisk and drizzle in half the olive oil. The liquid will emulsify. Pour in the balsamic vinegar and the remaining oil and leave the mixture in an airtight jar. Avoid putting it in the refrigerator – it's better kept at room temperature.

Just before serving, place the goat's cheese slices and the chopped walnuts on a non-stick baking tray under a hot grill and toast until the cheese starts to colour, blister and run. Be careful to ensure that the walnuts toast without burning.

Arrange a bed of salad leaves on each plate and use a spatula to lift the molten cheese onto them. Sprinkle over the walnuts. Give the dressing a vigorous whisk with a fork to combine all the elements and drizzle over the cheese, walnuts and leaves. Make sure that each plate has a combination of the flavoured oil, sweet vinegar and melt-in-the mouth shallot cream.

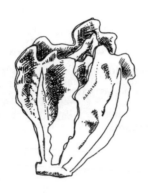

Spring onions

When it comes to spring onions, there are two types of people: those who relish the strong tasting white bulbs which add punch to a salad, and others who prefer the milder green stems. I tend to opt for the latter and inevitably end up with countless numbers of forlorn white bulbs in the refrigerator. Of course I find a use for them, usually in my 'Blow Your Mind' Salsa (see page 46) but it is the green stems that I relish first. I usually grow only a couple of clumps of spring onions and then overdose on them in just a few sittings. It's best to use them as soon as they are harvested; they have fabulous flavour and are the front line in the season's posse of alliums.

SCRAMBLED EGGS AND SPRING ONIONS ON SOURDOUGH TOAST

I love scrambled eggs. First, I like them to be scrambled – not beaten to death. Second, they must be a combination of only eggs and butter – no milk. And finally the eggs must be free-range. Here's my recipe for a perfect brunch.

SERVES 2

40g salted butter
5 large free-range eggs
6 spring onions, green ends
   only, chopped

2 slices sourdough bread
truffle oil (optional)
Parmesan (optional)
freshly ground black pepper

Melt half the butter in a non-stick saucepan on the lowest heat. Don't allow it to get too hot. Break the eggs into the pan one at a time. Break each yolk with a wooden spoon and give it a slow stir before adding the next egg. I like to see streaks of golden yellow and white, so although you should move the mixture around the pan, it doesn't need to be whisked. Add the remaining butter and let it melt and mingle with the eggs. Scatter the spring onions in the pan. While the eggs are cooking, make the toast. If you keep the heat low under the pan, there shouldn't be any crusty or dry bits; a little runny egg is ideal. Grind black pepper over the eggs in moderation, and serve the egg on top of the toast.

Variation: on special occasions I top with a drop or two of truffle oil or a grating of Parmesan.

STEAMED POLLACK WITH GINGER AND SPRING ONIONS

I definitely sense a physical change in myself in spring; a release for both mind and body from the imprisonment of the dark months of the year. Winter foods lose their appeal when all around nature has begun to stir. Quite why we have New Year's resolutions about eating more healthily and losing weight I never know; eating comfort food is what gets us through the winter. Spring would be a much better time than winter to try to lose a few pounds, eat lighter meals and maybe even wear a bit of Lycra for the occasional hour. I like to give my taste buds a wake up call when the spring onions are ready to harvest. Pollack is a superb alternative to cod. It has a meaty texture and really manages to absorb flavours, yet it is also delicate and shouldn't be overcooked.

SERVES 2

2 medium leeks, sliced lengthways

2cm knob ginger, peeled and finely choppped

2 cloves garlic, finely chopped

1 small red chilli, seeded and finely chopped

2 pollack or cod fillets (about 100g each)

juice 1 lime

50g spring onions, finely chopped

salt

dark soy sauce, to serve

baby rocket and baby spinach leaves, to serve

Take two squares of foil and place a bed of leek in the centre of each. Sprinkle over some of the ginger, garlic and chilli. Place the pollack fillets on top of this and cover them with the remaining chilli, garlic and ginger. Pour over the lime juice and sprinkle with salt. Fold up the foil to seal the parcels tightly. Put the parcels in a steamer for 15 minutes. (Alternatively bake on a tray in an oven heated to 220°C/200°C fan/425°F/ Gas mark 7 for 20 minutes.)

Open the foil parcels and sprinkle the spring onions over the pollack before taking the parcels to the table. Serve with a mound of rocket and baby spinach leaves and a drizzle of dark soy sauce.

The finish line is in sight

By the tail end of spring, just about every patch has been filled. There may still be a host of healthy seedlings in the greenhouse ready to plant in the ground, but soon the spring harvests will free up some space for planting. Every day grows longer and in a few weeks everything will find a place. It's an active time: tiny birds journey on an endless mission to keep their fledglings fed, bees and insects greedily search for nectar and there is still weeding to be done. Whether the sun shines, or misty rain falls, it's an idyllic scene. Every aching limb, sweaty brow or blistered hand has been worth it.

Occasionally the plot will need a hoe, but more often than not I just wander through the rows of emerging plants and think about what I will cook. Now is the time to chat to my allotment neighbours, complain about the crops that didn't make the cut and glory in those that did. The race may be over, but of course the real competition has only just begun.

Summer

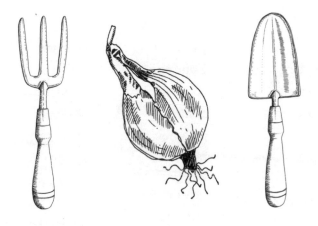

What to plant and harvest in summer

Continue to sow

beetroot	chard	radishes
carrots	peas	salad leaves

Harvest

basil	garlic	rhubarb
climbing beans	globe artichokes	rocket
celery	gooseberries	salad leaves
chard	onions	shallots
chillies	pak choi	spinach
chives	peas and pea shoots	sprouts
coriander	new potatoes	strawberries
courgettes	radishes	summer cabbage
cucumbers	raspberries	sweetcorn
fennel		tomatoes

SUMMER RECIPES

Beans

Sausage, beans and cheese

Simple borlotti stew

Courgettes

Courgette soup with feta and mint

Courgette and mint salad

Haddock with courgette ribbons, shallots and gooseberries

Courgette fritters with sunshine sauce

Cucumbers

Tuna with lime and cucumber

Cucumber raita

Edible flowers

Baby globe artichokes with bacon and citrus vinaigrette

Globe artichokes with butter, garlic and flat-leaf parsley

Lemon sole in lemon and chive butter

Spicy lamb burgers with flower salad

Garlic

Hummus

Chicken thighs with rosemary, lemon and garlic

Buttery spaghetti with garlic and sage

Summer herbs

Fennel and mint coleslaw

Sea bass fillet with braised fennel

Lemon chicken breast with tarragon hollandaise on green beans

*Pancetta-wrapped monkfish
with roast fennel and sweet potato chips*

Pak choi and summer cabbage

*Pork chops with wilted pak choi, chilli,
ginger, garlic and sesame oil*

Summer cabbage with Parmesan

Potatoes (earlies)

Warm potato salad with yoghurt dressing

Summer roast chicken with roasted new potatoes

Smashed new potatoes with bacon and cheese

Raspberries

Raspberry wobbles

Muesli with raspberries

Shallots

Anchovy, shallot and roasted garlic paste
Chorizo and shallots in cider vinegar
Roast fillet of beef with shallots in a creamy mushroom sauce

Strawberries

Strawberry and cream meringues
Salted strawberries
Strawberry and honey smoothie

Sweetcorn

Sweetcorn fritters with chilli and lime dressing
Chicken and sweetcorn soup

Tomatoes

Tomato and mozzarella salad
Tomato sauce (home and away) with spaghetti
Meatballs with tomato sauce
Italy on toast
Roast tomato soup with basil oil
Tomato chutney

They think it's all over...

It doesn't matter which month the calendar displays, or what the weather forecast predicts, nature alone decides when winter has ended and summer has begun. When it comes to seasons, missing out spring is not an error on my part. It's just that I see spring as a battleground between the two stronger and definitive seasons. In more recent times I have noticed that the weather in spring is much more extreme: it's a period when the weather can be wintry for three days, summery for two, then return to colder, windier, weather than we had during winter itself.

Summer makes itself known only when it is ready. Such unpredictability means that it's crucial that growers have a measured approach to the changing seasons. We need to notice details. We don't need the tabloids to proclaim, 'Phew what a scorcher' or to experience motorway traffic queues to know that it's summer. When you have picked the last of the purple sprouting broccoli and next year's seedlings are eager to be planted out, when the radishes and rocket are abundant and when the flowers appear on the strawberries, it's safe to say that summer is, at the very least, imminent.

The sun shines. Then, no sooner is a hosepipe ban announced than real summer, in all its precipitous glory, arrives. The vegetable plot will not wait though, so unless you don wellies and a raincoat and crack on, you will forever be playing catch-up. Pests and weeds try to assert themselves in the early summer, so it's important that you take charge and transplant the remainder of the eager seedlings before events spiral out of control. Digging gives way to hoeing. I will already have most of the plot planted by now, yet there are still key decisions to be made. Have I planted too much or too little for the space available? Do I have enough strong specimens of each variety, or have I been heavy on tomatoes and light on runner beans? Is my plot as good as it possibly can be? Can I squeeze in a little more of something? Should I take one last trip to the nursery? These are the things I don't mind worrying about.

This is a social time. There are plant swaps with allotment neighbours as you fill in the odd spot. There are usually plenty of spares to donate to friends, local fetes or passers-by, too. As the last emptied pot goes back into the shed, there is always, for me, a wonderful moment. Apart from a few seed drills here and there, the work is done. The plot looks at its most loved and all is well with the world. The early evening sun's rays illuminate the scene: newly fledged birds sing in the trees, insects fly, backlit by the evening sun and the vegetable oasis seems perfect. There's so much hope in the air and each new shoot is a joy. It's a time to feel energised and creative. Every row, every plant, every flower is a recipe-in-waiting – it's enough to send the taste buds into overdrive.

So, for a few balmy nights you may indulge in admiring the fruits of your endeavours. Wrestle out the chair that you stored at the back of the shed, sit with the evening birdsong and enjoy a beer or two. You have earned it.

The heaven is short lived. While early summer according to the calendar is mid-June, any Druid will tell you that midsummer is 21 June – the summer solstice and the longest day. Whilst the optimist in me sees this date as the day by which I want all my crops planted, my pessimistic alter ego reminds me that the days are about to get shorter and we are on the slippery slope to winter. Thankfully there is much to harvest between now and then. As I walk the narrow strips of grass between the beds I can only smile at the abundance, variety and quality of the crops beginning to grow. The days may grow shorter but they will also grow warmer. Every day for the next six months at least I will be constantly inspired and fed by the fruits of my labours.

Beans

....

Making a wigwam or tent of bamboo sticks is a calm and pleasurable task. It feels very British, or at least traditional, like Morris dancing or cricket on the village green.

Beans bring height to the allotment, and are one of the few crops you can harvest without getting muddy hands. I usually grow runners, French beans and borlottis.

Runner beans are fast. The trick is to pick them before the beans get too big. There's nothing worse than a stringy runner, so harvest when the beans are small and limp on the plant. The same is true of most beans. Unless you are leaving them to harvest the bean rather than the pod, the rule is the earlier you pick them the better. A side of steamed fresh new runners, French beans, yellow beans or borlottis laden with butter and garlic is a summer treat. I like to leave a few borlotti to harden off for a late summer stew but it's hard to resist picking them early.

SAUSAGE, BEANS AND CHEESE

I love this dish for its simplicity and the fact that my son Freddie is always eager to have sausage, beans and cheese, even when he finds out it's this version. He definitely tries and likes more vegetables as a result of the allotment.

SERVES 3

1 medium onion, chopped

10ml olive oil

100g chorizo, cut into
    bite-sized chunks

300g tomatoes, diced

150g runner beans, cut into
    bite-sized chunks

20ml balsamic vinegar

40g Parmesan, to serve

In a heavy-based saucepan soften the onion in the oil over a low heat, and add the chorizo chunks and tomatoes. Cook gently, allowing allow the juice of the tomatoes and sausage to mix. Add the beans to the simmering pan with the balsamic vinegar. Cover and continue to cook gently for about ten minutes. Serve with finely grated Parmesan. This is a delicious dish, perfect served with fluffy mash to soak up all the juices.

Variation: add a square of golden puff pastry to make a sausage and bean pie.

SIMPLE BORLOTTI STEW

Borlotti beans are so beautiful to look at, it's almost a shame to eat them. As with most beans, I try to eat the pods whole before the beans are really formed, but once they do start to firm up, I leave them till the end of the season and harvest them in one fell swoop. Of course harvesting in one go means podding in one go too. Freddie and I tend to sit on the back step and have father and son chats while we do it. Apparently he doesn't plan to get married because he wants to stay living with Mummy and Daddy. We'll see about that. I'm sure he'll change his mind when he's grown up. It won't be very practical living with us anyway, as according to him, he will be working as a superhero. I imagine that requires quite a bit of travel and late nights.

SERVES 3–4

400g borlotti beans

2 medium red onions, sliced

10ml olive oil

1 teaspoon cornflour

50ml red wine vinegar

300ml vegetable stock

200ml tomato passata

4 cloves garlic,
    roughly chopped

200ml white wine

1 celery stalk,
    roughly chopped

2 medium carrots,
    roughly chopped.

2 bay leaves

15g basil leaves

salt

extra-virgin olive oil, to serve

ciabatta bread, to serve

Preheat the oven to 170°C/150°C fan/325°F/Gas mark 3. Soak the beans for a good 12 hours in cold water, then drain and boil in salted water for about 40 minutes. (Or you could open a tin.) Soften the onion in the oil and then transfer to an ovenproof dish. Mix the cornflour with a little water and add with all the other ingredients except the basil. Cook slowly for about 90 minutes until the liquid is thick and viscous and the beans are soft. Finely chop the basil and add before serving. Serve with a good drizzle of extra-virgin olive oil and ciabatta bread.

Courgettes

....

Around the tail end of July, just as families start to disappear on their summer breaks, the mood on the plot takes a strange turn. The hollyhocks stand tall and sway in the evening breeze, beans reach for the skies and birds chatter in the low evening sun, but a recurring eerie sound shatters this idyll. Night after night, at around 7.30, a low groan breaks the serenity of the evening. The disturbing truth is that another grower has spotted yet more courgettes on the verge of marrowhood – the curse of the allotment holder.

Actually, I'm pretty fond of courgettes. At the beginning of the season when they are are small and sweet I eat them raw in salads, sautéed in butter and thrown into endless ratatouille-style dishes. As they grow bigger I still manage to enjoy them in other ways. By the time the summer sun is waning, I'm making soup and stuffing marrows.

There are a few alternative varieties that are worth growing. Yellow courgettes are pretty common now, and make a pleasant change. Rugosa is a pale, knobbly variety from Italy; it's a little firmer than most and has a nutty flavour. Custard whites, delicious baked and eaten whole when young, are also delightful when they grow bigger. Cut a lid in the top, remove the seeds, add some butter, thyme and grated Parmesan, then replace the lid and bake in a hot oven for around 40 minutes. The white flesh absorbs the flavours and is a lighter alternative to mashed potato.

COURGETTE SOUP WITH FETA AND MINT

This simple soup tastes outstanding and when you have courgettes coming out of your ears, it feels like an achievement to eat so many in one go. Anyone can make it and it freezes well too. I know that, like me, Natasha and Freddie both really enjoy this (daily) soup, although the question, 'How many courgettes did you use up?' does sometimes make me wonder if I should give them the weekends off.

SERVES 4–6

10ml vegetable oil

1 red onion, chopped

3 cloves garlic, chopped

1–2kg large courgettes, cut into big chunks

2 bay leaves

sprig thyme

2 tablespoons freshly squeezed lemon juice

salt and black pepper

15g mint, finely chopped

100g feta

drizzle extra-virgin olive oil

zest 1 unwaxed lemon

chive flowers, to garnish (optional)

Gently heat the oil in your largest saucepan. Add the onions, garlic and courgettes with a generous sprinkling of salt. Cover with a lid just smaller than the pan, so it rests on the mountain of courgettes, pressing them down. Keep the heat low and allow to cook for about ten minutes, stirring occasionally with a wooden spoon, so that all the courgette chunks get a turn at being on the bottom.

Add the bay leaves and the sprig of thyme and allow to cook gently for a further ten minutes. Pour in the lemon juice, then replace the lid for about 15 minutes. The courgette chunks will start to break down and release their moisture. When all the courgettes have softened, there will be a considerable amount of liquid in the pan. Remove the pan from the heat and liquidise the contents until the soup is smooth. The courgette skins will create dark speckles, making a great visual contrast to the almost luminous paler green.

Stir the mint into the soup before serving in individual bowls. Crumble a small handful of feta into the middle of each bowl, drizzle with the extra-virgin olive oil and finish with the lemon zest and a scattering of chive flowers, if you are using them.

Variations: try using a leek instead of the onion, or add a hunk of Parmesan rind to the soup mix and hold back on the salt. A few small chillies in the mix make it interesting; this is nice served with a dollop of Greek yoghurt or crème fraiche to take away the heat. It's also delicious chilled.

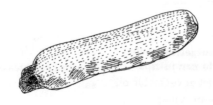

COURGETTE AND MINT SALAD

There are many good reasons to have an allotment: friendship and community come high on the list. I am blessed with the perfect horticultural neighbours. On the left there's Richard, who devotes so much time to his plots and grows (and knows) everything. On the right is Julie, who is consistently cheerful and optimistic. She always praises the positive aspects of my endeavours. Not only do I receive their generosity and encouragement on a regular basis, but when we have a glut of a particular crop, both offer their fair share of inspiration too. This courgette salad is based on one of Julie's. It is a wonderful dish for a summer's evening and yet another great way to deal with too many courgettes. The courgettes need to be cut thin enough to cook through quickly, though not so thin that they fall to pieces – around 4mm is ideal; you could use a mandoline to do this.

SERVES 2

4 medium courgettes, peeled and cut into 4mm strips
10ml rapeseed or vegetable oil
20ml white wine vinegar

20ml extra-virgin olive oil
handful mint leaves, chopped
salt

Lay the courgette strips on kitchen paper and sprinkle them with salt. Leave for at least ten minutes, then pat the strips dry with more kitchen paper.

Heat a griddle pan until it is searing hot and add the rapeseed or vegetable oil. Lay the courgettes on the griddle and cook them for about three minutes on each side until they are chargrilled. Remove and rest the slices on a large serving dish.

Drizzle the courgettes with equal quantities of white wine vinegar and extra-virgin olive oil. Sprinkle over the mint and a final grind of salt. Leave the salad to cool in the refrigerator. This is so delicious that you need little else, but it is also magical with a potato salad, a cucumber or radish tzatziki and a few tomatoes. Even if it's raining you will be transported to a sunny place.

HADDOCK WITH COURGETTE RIBBONS, SHALLOTS AND GOOSEBERRIES

Seeking a change from my ususal pairing of haddock with capers, I consulted the allotment. After a meander among the crops, I noticed that the courgettes (numerous varieties) were taking over (not unusual), that the harvested shallots were drying nicely in the sun and the gooseberry bushes were offering their first decent fruit of the summer. The slugs, meanwhile, seemed to be planning an assault on the pak choi. Thus were the ingredients for dinner chosen. The tart gooseberries in white wine vinegar enhance the flavour of the meaty fish without overpowering it. The best way to cut courgettes into ribbons is to use a vegetable peeler or mandoline.

SERVES 2

2 medium courgettes,
    cut into ribbons
6 small shallots,
    finely chopped
10ml olive oil
100g gooseberries,
    topped and tailed

2 haddock fillets
    (approx. 100g each)
sprig fennel
2 tablespoons white wine
    vinegar
200g pak choi, leaves
    separated and washed
salt

Sprinkle the courgette ribbons generously with salt and leave for ten minutes before dabbing dry with kitchen paper. In a large saucepan soften the shallots gently in the oil until translucent and add a sprinkling of salt. Turn up the heat to medium, add the courgettes and gooseberries and lay the fish fillets on top, topped with the fennel sprig. Pour in the white wine vinegar and cover the pan. Leave for about ten minutes, during which time the fish will steam as the gooseberries stew and the courgettes soften. Meanwhile, steam the pak choi over a pan of ferociously boiling water until it wilts. Serve the fish on a generous spoonful of the courgette, gooseberry and shallot mixture. Drizzle with the juices from the pan and serve the pak choi on the side.

COURGETTE FRITTERS WITH SUNSHINE SAUCE

This makes a delicious starter and, no matter how many fritters you make, they will all disappear. It's a wonderful dish to serve as part of a mezze too. On its own, the vibrant dipping sauce is a little intense, but combined with the fritters it packs just the right amount of punch.

SERVES 4 AS A STARTER

4 medium courgettes, peeled and cut into ribbons
vegetable oil, for deep frying

for the batter
290ml iced water
1 egg
130g plain flour
salt and pepper

for the sauce
1 medium red onion, chopped
2 cloves garlic, chopped
20ml olive oil, plus extra to cook the onion and garlic
70g sun dried tomatoes, finely chopped
10ml red wine vinegar
20g sugar
15g basil

Put the courgette ribbons in a colander and sprinkle with salt. Next prepare the batter. Mix the iced water, egg and half the flour into a smooth paste. Aim for a consistency between double and single cream: it needs to be thick enough to stick to the courgette ribbons, but not too thick. Put the batter to one side to rest and make the dipping sauce.

Soften the onion and garlic with a splash of oil in a saucepan over a low heat – you don't want them to colour. Add the sun dried tomatoes to the pan to warm through. Pour in the red wine vinegar and sugar and reduce the liquid by about a third. Turn off the heat. Chop most of the basil and add to the mix, pour in the olive oil, then blend in a food processor until smooth. Allow to cool.

Heat a heavy-based saucepan of vegetable oil over the highest heat. Pat the courgette ribbons as dry as possible with kitchen paper. Put the remaining flour and salt and pepper in a small freezer bag and add a handful of courgette ribbons. Give it a shake so the ribbons are lightly covered in flour. Then dip each ribbon in the batter to give it a very thin coating. Transfer them immediately to the pan of very hot oil, or a deep fryer. The fritters will cook in a few minutes and take on a beautiful golden hue. Carefully turn each fritter over half way through for an even colour. Put the fritters on kitchen paper to absorb any excess oil, then serve quickly as they are much more delicious when hot.

Tear the remaining basil and stir through the sauce immediately before serving. The courgettes will be sweet and chewy and the sauce fruity and tart.

Variation: if making a large quantity of fritters, try adding a teaspoon of paprika or cumin to the flour, once you have prepared some plain ones. You can also make this dish with aubergines and – if you are really daring – mix the two. This dish is also delicious with a garlic mayonnaise.

Cucumbers

Home-grown cucumbers are so different from their commercially-grown cousins. They are much less watery and have a really full flavour. Don't let them grow too big, as the skins thicken with age; pencil length is ideal. One plant will produce four or five fruits, so it's worthwhile finding a space in the greenhouse. They are sprawling plants and love to climb. I train them on a bamboo cane at a 45° angle so the cucumbers dangle down and are easy to pick.

TUNA WITH LIME AND CUCUMBER

I first tasted a version of this dish in a tiny restaurant in Tofino on Vancouver Island. I didn't ask for the recipe, just tried to work out how the chef had made it. The next day, still excited by the taste of the dish, I jotted down my thoughts, but subsequently lost the piece of paper. So this is probably nothing like the original and, by default, truly original. I plan to go back to Tofino one day and compare notes. You need to chop the tuna as finely as possible: my tip is to first cut the fish into strips with the grain and then to chop it into tiny chunks.

SERVES 4 AS A STARTER

2 tuna steaks (about 200g each), finely chopped

100g cucumber, peeled and finely chopped

4 shallots, finely chopped

juice 1 lime

20ml sherry vinegar

15ml olive oil

drizzle (5–10ml) truffle oil

salt

rocket leaves, to serve

thinly sliced cucumber, to serve

Mix the tuna with the cucumber and shallots in a bowl. Add the salt, lime juice, sherry vinegar and oils and mix. Put in the refrigerator for at least an hour and then squeeze out any excess moisture. Shape into small patties and serve with rocket leaves and thinly sliced cucumber.

CUCUMBER RAITA

A robust, home-grown cucumber is perfect for this dish. The yoghurt coats it beautifully, so it has crunch and yet delicacy in every mouthful. My spices may not be a traditional combination, but they work for me. I love the dance between coolness and heat in each mouthful.

SERVES 2

1 small cucumber (about 250g), peeled and very thinly sliced

3 teaspoons toasted cumin seeds

2 teaspoons hot chilli powder

3 teaspoons cinnamon

2 cloves garlic, thinly sliced

200g thick Greek yoghurt

salt and coarsely ground black pepper

20g mint, finely chopped, to serve

Sprinkle the sliced cucumber with a little salt and put it in a colander or sieve to allow excess moisture to drain off. Grind the cumin seeds in a pestle and mortar. Put the chilli powder, cumin, black pepper and cinnamon in a bowl with the cucumber. Crush the garlic to a paste, then combine with the yoghurt and stir into the other ingredients. Sprinkle with the mint before serving.

Edible flowers

The first time I saw someone eat a flower I was shocked, having been brought up never to eat anything other than a vegetable from the garden. Now I eat a wide variety of flowers. Nasturtiums, chive flowers and rose petals, together with young dandelion leaves, make an awesome salad. The velvety texture of nasturtium flowers is gentle and deceptive, as it's followed by a peppery hit. Bright blue borage flowers are good too, especially in a summer drink or cocktail.

Chives are another must-have edible flower. I grow as many as I can in a couple of huge pots. A mass of rich purple chive flowers in early spring brightens up the garden. Not only does the colour really sing, but a huge bold clump is also a magnet for bees. Two pots are essential: keep the first for the leaves and chop them short, and allow the second to flower. Once the flowers are over, use this as the main pot. The first pot will recover and reward you with a second wave of purple heads. The subtle and delicate flavour of the flower petals really bring a dish to life, while the long chive leaves bring both flavour and elegance to a dish.

Perhaps the ultimate edible flower is the globe artichoke. A perennial which doesn't need much attention, the plant almost disappears during the winter. By midsummer the blue-green leaves dominate their corner of the patch, taking up as much room as you are prepared to give them. The edible buds stand tall and noble and it's a wrench to cut them. Like most vegetables, they are better eaten young and small, although it's tempting to let a few reach maturity and flower. The fine purple petals are truly spectacular and worth sacrificing the odd meal for.

BABY GLOBE ARTICHOKES
WITH BACON AND CITRUS VINAIGRETTE

I harvest the globes young, when they are smaller than a tennis ball. There's a fair bit of waste, so the compost bin gains too. Eating an artichoke always feels like an event, however they are served. This combination of salty bacon, artichokes and citrus dressing looks magnificent on the plate and is endlessly satisfying on the palate.

SERVES 2

4 small globe artichokes, tough leaves and hairy chokes discarded, cut lengthways into quarters
100g smoked, fatty streaky bacon, cubed

juice ½ orange
6 sage leaves, finely chopped
50ml extra-virgin olive oil
salt

Bring a saucepan of salted water to the boil, put in the trimmed artichoke heads and cook for 8–10 minutes, then drain.

Fry the cubed bacon in its own fat over a medium–high heat until golden brown. Remove from the pan and set to one side. Turn up the heat. Lay the artichoke quarters cut side down in the pan for a few minutes to colour. Mix the orange juice, sage leaves and olive oil to make a dressing. Serve each artichoke heart with a scattering of bacon and a generous drizzle of the dressing.

GLOBE ARTICHOKES WITH BUTTER, GARLIC AND FLAT-LEAF PARSLEY

You need to pick the artichokes for this dish at the right time: when they are fist size they will be perfect. If the purple petals have started to appear, just leave them to flower. Sitting in full sun, peeling off the soft artichoke leaves and dipping them in garlic and parsley butter is delightful. It's one of the things I daydream about in the cold, damp winter and when the occasion arrives it never fails to please.

SERVES 2

2 large globe artichokes
1 clove garlic, finely chopped
10g flat-leaf parsley, finely chopped
100g salted butter, slightly softened
salt

Snip off the sharp points of the artichoke leaves. Use a teaspoon to scoop out and discard as much of the hairy choke from the centre of the flower as you can. Bring a large saucepan of salted water to the boil, and cook the artichokes for 30 minutes, or longer if they are larger or older.

Mix the garlic and parsley into the softened butter, then put it in the refrigerator to firm up. If you are cooking to impress, roll it into a sausage shape in cling film, tighten the ends and pop into the freezer for 20 minutes. You will then be able to cut neat slices to serve. Alternatively spoon a blob of butter onto the side of each plate and serve with the steaming hot artichokes.

LEMON SOLE IN LEMON AND CHIVE BUTTER

Chive flowers have such a delicate flavour and look fantastic. This is a quick and satisfying dish to make on a sunny early summer evening. When you eat it, all of a sudden winter feels a long way away and everything feels right with the world. You can use any flat fish, and plaice works just as well as sole.

SERVES 2

40g butter
2 lemon sole fillets (150g each)
juice and zest 1 unwaxed lemon, curled
10g chives, chopped
3 or 4 chive flowers, to serve

Melt the butter in a saucepan until it just starts to bubble, then reduce the heat. Put the sole fillets in the pan, skin side down, and allow them to sizzle for a minute. Pour in the lemon juice and put a lid over the fish. (I have a wide saucepan and use the lid of my steamer, which fits inside the pan and seals in the steam.) After about five minutes add the chives and allow them to warm through before transferring the sole fillets to a warm serving plate. Drizzle over the chives and juices from the pan. Finish with a scattering of petals from the chive flowers and a couple of curls of lemon zest.

Variation: if you don't have chive flowers, try deep frying thin strands of leek. Or if you prefer to use flowers, add some nasturtium petals.

SPICY LAMB BURGERS
WITH FLOWER SALAD

This is a fantastic dish for one of those summer Saturdays when friends are coming round with a few bottles of wine. The main preparation is completed in advance so there is little to be done apart from picking the salad. This dish is truly memorable, both visually and in terms of flavour. Once you've tried it, no matter how much wine you later regret drinking, you will remember the sight, smell and taste of it with affection. Kids relish eating the flowers.

SERVES 6–8

for the burgers

10g each coriander, mustard and cumin seeds
500g lamb mince
1 large onion, finely chopped
4 anchovy fillets, finely chopped
40g mint, finely chopped
2 small chillies, finely chopped
4 cloves garlic, finely chopped
100g breadcrumbs
1 egg, beaten

for the salad

a selection of salad leaves: wild rocket, young dandelion, mizuna, baby beetroot, red sorrel, spinach and mustard leaves
edible flowers

for the dressing

250ml plain yoghurt
20g mint leaves, chopped
juice ½ lime
1 teaspoon harissa
50ml olive oil

In a heavy frying pan, gently toast the coriander, mustard and cumin seeds, before pounding them in a pestle and mortar. Add the spice mix to the lamb mince, onion, anchovies, mint, chilli and garlic in a large bowl. Add the breadcrumbs and the egg and mix together. Roll the mixture into even sized burgers (plus a few smaller ones if you're feeding kids) and rest them in the refrigerator.

Assemble the salad leaves, adding some nasturtium flowers for peppery zing and chive flowers for sweetness and vibrancy. Combine all the ingredients for the dressing.

Cook the burgers under a hot grill for no more than ten minutes per side (a little less if you like them pink). They are also delicious barbequed. Serve on a mound of the salad and top with the dressing.

Variation: these burgers are also good with home-made coleslaw (see page 99), or topped with a dollop of hummus (see page 95). You could push the boat out with a potato salad (see page 109). Tarragon instead of mint in the burgers works well too.

Garlic

When I've finished harvesting the garlic and have tray upon tray drying in my garage, even the proudest French chef would be aromatically impressed. I love garlic. I love eating it, cooking with it and growing it. It's a confident bulb and I have much luck cultivating it. I usually try a few varieties: mainly Solent Wight for a continuous supply, Elephant garlic for its ridiculously large yet milder cloves and Lautrec pink garlic for its French name, deep flavour (and scapes, or flower stalks). Freshly harvested (green) garlic is juicier and less pungent. As the bulb dries through late summer and autumn the flavour becomes much more intense, so you need to use less.

HUMMUS

This recipe needs a warning: once you've tasted it you'll no longer be satisfied with supermarket hummus – it's just not in the same league. This hummus is light, full of flavour and can be adapted to make different versions. It's also incredibly easy to make and takes little time from start to finish.

SERVES 4–6

500g dried chickpeas
(or 2 × 400g cans chickpeas, drained)
3 cloves garlic
2 teaspoons ground cumin
(or cumin seeds)
2 teaspoons hot chilli powder

60–70ml sunflower oil
30g tahini
40ml freshly squeezed
lemon juice
60–70ml extra-virgin olive oil
60–70ml water
salt

Soak the dried chickpeas in a large saucepan of water for at least 12 hours (they will absorb water and become heavier). The next day, drain and rinse them several times. Cover them in fresh water and salt generously. Bring to the boil and simmer for about 40 minutes, until the chickpeas are soft but not disintegrating. If you use a pressure cooker it will take about half the time. Drain and rinse.

Put the garlic, a pinch of salt, the cumin, chilli powder and a drizzle of sunflower oil in a food processor and blitz them to a paste. Add the tahini, half the chickpeas, the lemon juice and olive oil and blitz again. Then add the rest of the chickpeas. This time as you blitz, slowly drizzle in the rest of the sunflower oil and water; personal taste dictates the consistency. The quantities above make a hummus with the perfect thickness to be lifted on a crisp.

Variation: if you prefer a richer flavour, add more olive oil and less water. I often make larger quantities, then split the final mix into three and add extra chilli powder to one, more cumin to another and some zest and extra lemon juice to the third.

CHICKEN THIGHS WITH ROSEMARY, LEMON AND GARLIC

This dish is worth cooking for the aroma alone: the combination of roasting chicken and the Mediterranean waft of rosemary and garlic creates a smell to make the kitchen smile. It's a dish which needs plenty of garlic and a lot of rosemary and is equally delicious served with either roast potatoes or a salad. Your rosemary bush needs to be big and robust enough to cut a bouquet from it without killing the plant.

SERVES 4

12 or more generous sprigs woody rosemary
8 chicken thighs (skin on)
12 cloves garlic, peeled and left whole

20ml olive oil
20ml lemon juice
salt and black pepper

Preheat the oven to 200°C/180°C fan/400°F/Gas mark 6. Put the rosemary in the bottom of a large roasting tin. Lay the chicken thighs on top and poke in a garlic clove or two beside each one. Drizzle with oil, a sprinkling of salt and a splash of lemon juice and roast for half an hour. The rosemary will singe as it cooks, and the flavour will infuse the meat as well as the kitchen.

Increase the oven temperature to 220°C/200°C fan /425°F/Gas mark 7 for the last ten minutes to crisp the chicken skin. Transfer the thighs to a serving dish and sprinkle with a little more lemon juice, salt and pepper before serving.

BUTTERY SPAGHETTI
WITH GARLIC AND SAGE

This is a dinner for when you're feeling lazy. It's ideal for those nights when you have no food in the house and for those times when you really can't face cooking. I'm not sure it's the kind of dish you should serve other people, but when you're home alone it's a perfect treat.

SERVES 1

75g spaghetti
60g unsalted butter
2 cloves garlic, finely chopped

4 large sage leaves,
   finely chopped
salt

Heat a large saucepan of water to boiling point and put in the spaghetti and some salt. Cook the spaghetti according to the packet instructions. Meanwhile, slowly melt the butter in a large frying pan and gently cook the garlic in it. Drain the spaghetti and add to the pan of garlic butter. Turn off the heat and cover the pan. Toss the sage leaves through the buttery pasta before serving.

Summer herbs

Some herbs add a subtle flavour to a dish; others are so loud that they define the recipe. These are the herbs I call the grown-ups, such as tarragon, fennel and mint.

Tarragon is a must, either English or French (perhaps even the milder Russian). I have a couple of healthy pots. Every summer I bury the pots in the ground, so I don't have to worry about them drying out; the plants draw all the moisture they need from the soil. Then, as autumn bites, I dig the pots out to overwinter in the greenhouse. The plants lie dormant until spring but do need that protection from frost.

I'm a bit scared of mint. I think that's because I was told as a child how it can spread and take over gardens. I have worried about it subconsciously ever since. Because of this fear, I have been nervous about planting it. As a result, I tend to keep it in a pot, at most planting the pot in the soil. The trouble is, mint just doesn't grow with the same ferocity if the roots are restrained. So this year I've faced my demons and planted a few varieties straight in the soil. So far, they have behaved; although they have provided me with an infinitely better crop than mint in pots, they haven't yet invaded. Of course I do watch them closely. Brushing past a confident shrub, for some reason, always whisks me back to childhood. Probably that very same moment when I was told that it 'takes over'. Phobia aside, I have noticed that I use mint more frequently these days.

Fennel looks fantastic in a flower bed. The feathery leaves add delicacy and interest when it's planted among bright poppies and nasturtiums. The fine foliage is wonderful with fish, the seeds make a great base for a curry and the bulb oozes flavour and elegance on the plate.

FENNEL AND MINT COLESLAW

Home-made coleslaw is fantastic. I usually use a food processor for speed, though a good sharp knife and a chopping board are a therapeutic alternative. The combination of vegetables is a matter of personal taste, but it's good to use a variety of colours, flavours, textures and sizes. I like to use fennel and mint as they are so distinctive and fresh; cabbage is also essential. Everything else can be added depending on whim or availability.

SERVES 8

½ red cabbage,
   finely shredded
½ white cabbage,
   finely shredded
1 fennel bulb, finely shredded
4 large carrots, grated
2 medium courgettes,
   cut into small chunks
1 red onion, thinly sliced

2 sticks celery,
   plus a few celery leaves
1 apple, grated
20ml lemon juice
300ml plain yoghurt
1 tablespoon Dijon mustard
80ml olive oil
30g mint, chopped
salt and black pepper

Put all the vegetables and fruit into a large bowl, pour over the lemon juice and add a generous pinch of salt. Mix everything well; the lemon juice will prevent everything turning brown.

Mix together the yoghurt, mustard and oil in a bowl and combine with the vegetables and fruit. A final scattering of mint adds a welcome surprise to every mouthful. This will keep in a sealed plastic container in the refrigerator for a couple of days.

Variation: try using roots such as kohlrabi, celeriac and parsnip to vary the flavour. Chop them finely and use less of them than the other main ingredients.

SEA BASS FILLET WITH BRAISED FENNEL

This is a refreshing al fresco mid-week treat. The need for a couple of glasses of white wine inevitably means you will want to finish the bottle, and if the sun is shining, quite possibly a second bottle. It always feels like a good idea at the time.

Soft buttery fennel, delicate white fish and a sweet tomato sauce make the last rays of a day's sunshine even more pleasurable. Even when the sun sets, the warming fennel allows you to enjoy being out of doors for a while longer. Before you know it, you'll be sitting under a summer moon lost in the moment. A magical dish.

SERVES 2

20ml olive oil

1 onion, finely chopped

2 cloves garlic, finely chopped

2 glasses white wine

500g overripe tomatoes, roughly chopped

4 anchovy fillets, finely chopped

50g salted butter

1 fennel bulb, thinly sliced

200g spinach, roughly chopped

2 sea bass fillets (about 150g each)

3 tablespoons capers

20g basil leaves, torn

salt

olive oil, for drizzling

unwaxed lemon zest, grated, to serve

Heat the oil in a heavy-bottomed saucepan and sauté the onion and garlic for a few minutes until soft. Turn up the heat and add a glass of white wine; let it bubble for a moment or two and then add the tomatoes and anchovies. Once bubbling, reduce to a gentle heat and simmer for 15 minutes.

Melt the butter in another saucepan and add the fennel slices, a pinch of salt, the second glass of white wine and the same amount of water. Cover and cook over a low heat for about 15 minutes until all the liquid is absorbed and the fennel is soft and translucent.

Add the spinach to the tomato sauce, then place the fish fillets carefully on top of the sauce and cover the saucepan with a lid. The fish will cook through in about five minutes. Use a fish slice to transfer the sea bass to a plate. Add the capers and basil leaves to the sauce and stir.

Serve in bowls with the fish on top of the sauce and the fennel on the side. Give each bowl a drizzle of olive oil and a grating of lemon zest and eat straight away.

LEMON CHICKEN BREAST WITH TARRAGON HOLLANDAISE ON GREEN BEANS

Chicken and tarragon are such a perfect combination; lemon and garlic add to the experience and the beans complete the party. If you can pick the beans just before cooking them, all the better. You will need a two-tier steamer for this dish.

SERVES 2

2 chicken breasts
(about 150g each)

4 cloves garlic,
peeled and halved

30g tarragon leaves

1 unwaxed lemon,
thickly sliced

200g green beans, sliced
diagonally in 2cm slices

for the hollandaise

125g butter

2 egg yolks

10g tarragon, finely chopped

10ml lemon juice

salt and freshly ground
white pepper

Slice into the chicken breasts to make a pocket in each and pack these with the garlic. On the lower level of a steamer lay half the tarragon, then position the chicken breasts on top. Lay the lemon slices on top of the chicken, and finish with another layer of tarragon. Put a blanket of foil over the top and tuck it in tightly, so the chicken doesn't dry out. Steam for ten minutes.

Put the beans in the top tier of the steamer. Remove the foil from the chicken and steam the beans and chicken for a further ten minutes while you make the hollandaise.

For the hollandaise, gently melt the butter in a saucepan. Whisk the egg yolks in a bowl over a pan of simmering water. You don't want them to cook too quickly; you are aiming for a light golden foam, not scrambled eggs. Remove from the heat and gently and slowly drizzle in the butter, whisking as you go. The sauce will thicken and glisten. Add the tarragon leaves to the sauce with the lemon juice and a sprinkling of salt and pepper. Serve the chicken on a mound of beans, drizzled with the hollandaise.

PANCETTA-WRAPPED MONKFISH WITH ROAST FENNEL AND SWEET POTATO CHIPS

*Every time I see a monkfish on a slab of ice in the fishmonger's,
I imagine what a terrifying experience it must have been the first
time a fisherman ever caught one. It's such a scary looking fish I think
I might just have let it go out of fear. Monkfish is one of my favourite
fish; it is so firm and meaty and yet delicate too. The flavours in this
dish work together well and the succulent fish looks splendid.*

SERVES 2

1 fennel bulb, thinly sliced

20ml olive oil

20ml aniseed liqueur,
    such as pastis or ouzo

1 large sweet potato (about
    200g), peeled and cut into
    chunky chips

10ml rapeseed oil

1 teaspoon paprika

6 thin rashers smoked
    pancetta

2 monkfish tails
    (about 150g each), deboned

2 sage leaves

30g unsalted butter

seasalt flakes and pepper

Preheat the oven to 200°C/180°C fan/400°F/Gas mark 6.
Put the fennel in a roasting dish, add the oil and liqueur and
mix thoroughly. Sprinkle with the seasalt flakes. Cover with
a blanket of foil to stop the fennel burning and to encourage
steam. Pop in the oven for 30 minutes.

Put the sweet potato pieces in a bowl along with the
rapeseed oil, paprika and salt and pepper. Mix carefully to
ensure that each chip is evenly coated. Heat an ovenproof,
non-stick frying pan, and when it is piping hot, put in the
chips and colour them on all sides, turning them carefully.
Once the outside of each chip is sealed, carefully transfer
the pan to the oven for 20 minutes.

Lay the pancetta slices at a 45° angle on a board and
wrap the monkfish tails tightly in them, adding the sage
leaves between the fish and the ham. Make sure the monkfish
is completely covered, so it doesn't dry out. Remove the foil

from the fennel and put the monkfish parcels on top of the fennel (so it's not swimming in the juice). Push some fennel around the fillets too. Add the butter and bake for 15 minutes in the hot oven.

To serve, criss-cross half the caramelised sweet potato chips in the centre of each plate and pile a generous mound of soft fennel over them. Rest the monkfish parcels on top and drizzle the buttery aniseed sauce over everything.

Pak choi and summer cabbage

I succeeded in growing my first pak choi crop this year – it seems to be a slug magnet, the birds organise frenzied attacks on the outer leaves, and I haven't grown it successfully before. On the plate, it is full of flavour and it should only ever be cooked briefly. Pak choi starts the summer as a salad vegetable – tasty leaves and refreshing stems that add flavour and crunch to any salad. As they grow bigger they need to be wilted or steamed, but very lightly: the joy is in the crunch.

I also look forward to summer cabbage. Crisp, pale green and dense, it is surprisingly delicate in the pan. A spring or summer cabbage should be cooked in very little water – just a splash – and some butter, salt and pepper; it poaches and steams rather than boils.

PORK CHOPS WITH WILTED PAK CHOI, CHILLI, GINGER, GARLIC AND SESAME OIL

Pork and cabbage complement each other well and the Asian elements in this dish tie the flavours together. The dish is all about timing and speed, so prepare all the vegetables before you start cooking.

SERVES 2

10ml rapeseed oil
2 pork chops (about 250g each)
20ml cider vinegar
2 cloves garlic, finely chopped

1 medium red chilli, finely chopped
2cm piece root ginger, finely chopped
200g pak choi, washed
10ml sesame oil

Put the rapeseed oil in a frying pan over a high heat and cook the chops for 3–4 minutes on each side. Don't worry if they turn golden on the outside and stick to the pan; a little caramelisation is fine. Once they are cooked through, put them to one side to rest.

Now work fast: turn the heat down to very low and deglaze the pan with the cider vinegar. As it reduces add the garlic, chilli and ginger. After a couple of minutes, turn off the heat, pop in the pak choi and cover the pan. The pak choi will wilt in moments. Add a drizzle of sesame oil to the pan and serve the chops on top of the wilted pak choi, with the pan juices poured over the top.

SUMMER CABBAGE WITH PARMESAN

This modest dish has real presence. A tightly packed, pale white cabbage has immense flavour and in this dish the cabbage is the centre of attention. On first bite the strands of cabbage seem very delicate, but the crunch is still there. The Parmesan, garlic, lemon and thyme transform an ordinary ingredient into a real treat. This is a wonderful snack on its own, but also ideal if you are having a few small plates.

SERVES 4

1 white cabbage,
   very thinly sliced
juice and zest ½ unwaxed
   lemon
2 sprigs thyme, leaves very
   finely chopped

1 clove garlic,
   very finely chopped
20ml extra-virgin olive oil
30g Parmesan
black pepper

Put the cabbage in a large bowl. Chop the lemon zest and mix with the thyme leaves and garlic. Drizzle the olive oil and the lemon juice over the cabbage. Grate the Parmesan into the bowl and add the garlic, zest and thyme. Mix to distribute the flavours evenly. Serve with a grinding of black pepper.

Potatoes

....

For me, nothing really beats a potato. They may be portrayed as the carb criminals of many a modern diet, but life without a jacket, a chip or a butter-laden new potato is not really a life is it? In fact the spud is packed full of vitamins and minerals.

There are so many varieties, each with its own strengths and window of perfection that just saying 'potato' is equivalent to calling all vehicles cars. I'm not suggesting that everyone dons an anorak and becomes a culinary trainspotter, but if you want to get the best out of spuds, it's worth getting to know them. I plant several varieties: some salad potatoes, such as Charlotte and Pink Fir Apple; early new varieties such as Pentland Javelin and Red Duke of York; plus a good selection of maincrop potatoes such as King Edward, Desiree or Arran Victory. The later varieties have more starch, a more floury texture and are left in the ground to grow bigger. The earlier types are often described as firm and waxy.

There is little you can do on the plot that is more satisfying than harvesting potatoes. It's like digging for gold. Forking carefully through the dark earth to reveal little balls of flavour that glow against the black earth is part of the magic of gardening; the only greater pleasure is to eat them.

WARM POTATO SALAD
WITH YOGHURT DRESSING

This potato salad accompanied by a few crisp salad leaves is a magnificent end to a day's harvesting and weeding. It has a pure flavour and a freshness that is always a delight. Use small waxy new potatoes such as Pink Fir Apple or Charlotte.

SERVES 6

2kg new potatoes, washed, cut into similar size pieces
salt

for the dressing

**1 medium red onion,
  finely chopped**
1 clove garlic, thinly sliced
250g Greek yoghurt
2 tablespoons Dijon mustard

100ml olive oil
**juice and zest 1 unwaxed
  lemon**
chive leaves and flowers

Boil the potatoes for 10–15 minutes in a large saucepan of generously salted water. When a sharp knife pierces a potato easily, drain and cover them so they continue to steam while you prepare the dressing.

Put the onion and garlic in a large bowl and add the yoghurt, mustard and oil. Mix well. Keep stirring and add a generous splash of lemon juice. Pour the dressing over the steaming potatoes, ensuring that each one is coated in the creamy mixture. To serve, add a generous scattering of chive leaves and flowers and the lemon zest. This is delicious eaten warm or chilled.

Variation: for an even simpler, lighter dressing, combine finely chopped fresh mint and flat-leaf parsley with olive oil, lemon juice and rock salt. The vibrant flavour makes a stunning summer evening dish.

SUMMER ROAST CHICKEN
WITH ROASTED NEW POTATOES

There's something very indulgent about serving a roast chicken
at the height of summer. Yet the aroma of a bronzing bird packed
with summer herbs and garlic is heavenly. Add a tray of crisp roast
new potatoes cooked just hours after being harvested and this dish
becomes a treat. Then there is the bonus that the evenings are long
enough to eat outdoors. Tucking into second helpings, with the sun
going down and the wine and conversation flowing is no better denial
of the working week's eve.

When it comes to chicken I'm a great believer that you only get
out what you put in. Nowadays it's socially unacceptable to buy any
chicken that hasn't had a charmed life, but often the cost of the most
privileged birds makes them beyond all pockets, bar the affluent. I do
hope all those posh chickens find homes; it would be a terrible shame
if they priced themselves out of the market. We all have our price, so
buy the best chicken you can afford and I'm convinced that as long
as you pack it with flavour and don't let it dry out, you won't get
anything other than smiles at the table.

From a flavour point of view I like my summer roasts to be light
and fresh: lemon, garlic and plenty of herbs are the secret. It's a good
idea to vary the herbs depending on which plant looks most abundant
at the time. I prefer not to mix the herbs, rather to go for a distinctive
flavour. My first choice is usually thyme, with tarragon coming a
close second. Roasted in this way, the flavour from inside the chicken
oozes into the liquid around it. This prevents the onions burning and
produces steam in the oven to prevent the chicken from drying out.
As the liquid reduces, so do the onions, leaving a fabulous foundation
for a gravy.

Roasted new potatoes bring a delight of their own. Pink Fir Apples
are exceptional when roasted, partly because of their slightly nutty
flavour, but also because cut lengthways, the potatoes make fantastic
shapes on the plate. Charlottes, Red Duke of Yorks or any small waxy
new potato work well though.

SERVES 4

for the chicken
- 1 lemon, halved
- 1 chicken (about 2kg)
- big bunch (about 20g) thyme or tarragon
- 2 bay leaves
- ½ bulb garlic, cloves unpeeled and left whole
- 5 medium onions, 1 halved and 4 roughly chopped
- 20ml olive oil
- 200ml dry white wine
- 200ml water
- salt

for the potatoes and green veg
- 1kg new potatoes
- 100ml rapeseed oil
- 10 shallots, peeled
- 4 cloves garlic, skins on
- 300g runner beans, sliced, or 200g spinach leaves
- olive oil for drizzling
- 10ml lemon juice
- salt

Preheat the oven to 200°C/180°C fan/400°F/Gas mark 6. Put half the lemon inside the bird, and pack in a generous bunch of thyme or tarragon, two bay leaves and the garlic cloves. Squeeze in two halves of onion and then the other half of the lemon. Rub the chicken with olive oil and sprinkle generously with salt, to dry the skin and make it crisp. Place the chicken in a roasting tin on a bed of chopped onions. Finally, pour in equal measures of wine and water – roughly a cup of each should provide enough liquid to almost cover the onion but not touch the bird. Cook for about 1½ hours, checking that there is still enough liquid in the tin after an hour. Remove the chicken from the oven and rest on a warmed serving dish. Cover with foil.

Put the potatoes in a large saucepan of salted water, bring it rapidly to the boil and cook for five minutes. The aim is to soften, not completely cook, the potatoes. While they are boiling, heat a baking tray with the rapeseed oil on the top shelf of the oven. Drain the potatoes and lay them cut side up in the hot oil. Sprinkle with salt and put the tray back in the oven for ten minutes. Take out the tray and give the potatoes a shake, this time arranging them cut side down. Add the shallots and garlic, and pop the tray back in the oven for 20 minutes. When the shallots and garlic have softened and the potatoes have crisp exteriors and soft centres, remove and transfer to a warm serving dish, leaving as much oil in the pan as possible.

Boil a small amount of water in a saucepan and pop in the runner beans or wilt the spinach leaves. Soften, but don't overcook them. Drain, reserving the vegetable water, and put them in a serving dish, drizzling over a dash of olive oil and a splash of lemon juice. Keep warm in the oven.

Pour off any excess oil from the roasting tin, then add a ladle or two of the vegetable water. Turn up the heat and scrape any sticky bits off the base of the tin to make sure that all the flavours from the pan are absorbed. Strain the gravy and serve.

SMASHED NEW POTATOES WITH BACON AND CHEESE

To enjoy new potatoes at their best you need to get them on the plate as soon as possible after harvesting: 15 minutes from plot to plate is ideal. Use small potatoes or cut in half any that are larger than a golf ball.

SERVES 3

750g baby new potatoes
150g fatty streaky bacon, cubed
50g Parmesan, finely grated
salt and black pepper

Boil the potatoes in salted water until they are cooked through; just over ten minutes. While they are cooking, crisp the bacon cubes in a hot, heavy frying pan (you won't need oil). Drain the potatoes and break them up with a fork – don't mash them, just crack or smash them enough to absorb the fat as you tip them into the frying pan with the bacon. Turn off the heat and sprinkle the Parmesan over the top. Flash under a hot grill to melt the cheese and serve immediately with a grind or two of black pepper.

Raspberries

I netted my raspberries this year. Last year they got away. The angry birds meant I wasn't able to harvest a single berry, let alone make a pavlova. Netting may sound like an easy pastoral task, but raspberries tend to grow rather randomly, and I guess I was a bit random in my approach to the job. The net result was that several plants remained outside the cordon. Freddie, who was an innocent four-year-old, believed that I deliberately planted some 'for the birds'. I didn't correct him. In one moment I was transformed from a horticultural failure to a benefactor of nature, custodian of the countryside and warrior for wildlife, without uttering a sound. Like strawberries, raspberries benefit from a quick transition from plot to plate, but even the less perfect specimens have their uses.

RASPBERRY WOBBLES

Raspberries are delicate fruits and when Freddie and I pick them we always have two bowls – one for the ripe and firm berries; the other for the slightly overripe and mushy ones. Of course the mushy ones are bursting with flavour, so here is a recipe for a dessert that uses up every last one. You will have some egg whites left over; you can use these to make Strawberry and Cream Meringues (see page 124).

SERVES 4

350g squishy raspberries, washed

3 tablespoons water

70g caster sugar

100g granulated sugar

300ml full fat milk

250ml single cream

2 eggs plus 3 extra yolks

Before you start, put four ramekins or dariole moulds in the refrigerator to chill. Preheat the oven to 170°C/150°C fan/ 325°F/Gas mark 3.

Put the raspberries in a saucepan with a tablespoon of water and 20g of the caster sugar and heat gently. The raspberries will gradually break down and produce a delicious syrup. Strain, and set the syrup and raspberries to one side.

In a saucepan gently heat the granulated sugar with two tablespoons of water and two tablespoons of the raspberry syrup. Increase the heat as the sugar starts to melt so that it bubbles into a thick caramel. Don't let it burn. Remove the pan from the heat. Pour a little raspberry-infused caramel into each ramekin and put to one side to set.

Meanwhile, put the milk, cream and the remaining 50g of caster sugar into a saucepan over a low heat, and melt the sugar. Stir, cover and remove from the heat. Allow the mixture to cool for half an hour.

In a bowl beat together the eggs and the egg yolks thoroughly. Slowly pour in the warm milk mixture and stir. Carefully spoon the mixture into the ramekins. Put the ramekins in an oven dish and fill the dish with hot water until it comes up to three quarters of the way up the sides of the ramekins. Cover with a piece of foil and bake for 40 minutes.

Remove the ramekins from the oven and put them to one side to cool before putting them in the refrigerator to set fully, which will take at least two hours. Tip out on to serving plates, put the raspberries on top and drizzle over any remaining syrup.

MUESLI WITH RASPBERRIES

On its own this muesli is heavenly. A handful of fresh raspberries make it a superb start to the culinary day. I must admit I never imagined that I would make my own muesli; life surely is too short? However, I became fed up with the sweetness and monotony of shop-bought museli – and indeed its high price tag. So I tried it making it; and now I'm hooked. Since I've been making my own breakfast, I'm a convert to the idea that the first mouthfuls of food each morning set the tone for the day.

It's a hard dish to wean yourself off though. You may well find, from now on, that every Sunday afternoon involves making muesli – and when you are asked what you did at the weekend, I warn you that 'making muesli' does sound just a tad middle class and middle aged. It may not be too late to join the Bridge Club.

Oats are essential – not just for flavour and texture, but also for economy. The combination of nuts and seeds is up to you. I like to include cashews, almonds and sunflower seeds; walnuts and chopped hazelnuts are good too.

MAKES 30 SERVINGS

375g dates	**100g seeds**
6 tablespoons clear honey	**100ml groundnut oil**
600g giant rolled oats	**2 teaspoons salt**
500g nuts, whole or in pieces	**50g raspberries, to serve**

Put the dates and a little water in a saucepan over a low heat and stew them until soft. Add the salt, along with the honey, then blitz with a hand whisk. The mixture doesn't have to be completely smooth. Pour it into a large bowl and add the dry ingredients and the oil. Mix thoroughly before spreading the mixture evenly on a non-stick baking tray. Toast under a hot grill for a few minutes until golden, turning over the mixture halfway. Remove and preheat the oven to its lowest setting and bake for half an hour. Cool and store in an airtight container. Freshly picked raspberries will make this taste even better.

Shallots

....

Harvesting shallots is really rewarding. For every bulb planted, you will harvest perhaps ten or more, if conditions are right. The outer skin is always delicate, but don't flake it off as you harvest; it's better to let the shallots dry in the sun. The papery thin wrapping helps to keep the flavour in, diseases out and preserves the shallots for months.

I once resided in a village where there were a few growers who lived for the annual village show. I was never particularly excited or challenged by the prospect of entering vegetables. 'Three potatoes of regular shape and size on a plate' or 'longest parsnip' weren't badges I felt the need to own. For others though, the village show was an annual battle and they would go to any lengths to get the most rosettes and their name on a trophy. I remember that one exhibitor let me into the secret of perfect shallot skins. The trick was to bury the shallots in a shoe box full of talcum powder for three weeks before the competition and then to brush off the powder with a paintbrush the night before the show. He then used a magnifying glass and tweezers to peel off any damaged layers and reveal his perfect, prize-winning shallots. If anyone wants to peel the layers off that onion, feel free.

ANCHOVY, SHALLOT AND ROASTED GARLIC PASTE

I'm a bit of an anchovy fan, but alas the only one in the house, which means I have to sneak them into dishes, or eat a whole tin myself as a little extra snack. After making a small Caesar salad for lunch one day, I was contemplating scoffing the rest of the tin when I spotted some shallots in the veg rack and put this recipe together. Spread thinly on toast, this is divine, but for ultimate satisfaction, serve with a lamb chop.

SERVES 2

10 medium shallots
1 medium bulb garlic
20ml olive oil
20ml balsamic vinegar

10 anchovy fillets,
 half finely chopped
100g unsalted butter
30ml ruby port

Preheat the oven to 170°C/150°C fan/325°F/Gas mark 3. Leave the shallots and garlic cloves in their skins and rub them with the oil and then the vinegar. Roast them in an ovenproof dish for half an hour.

Remove the dish from the oven and leave it to cool. Squeeze the paste from the roasted garlic and shallots into a small saucepan. Add the chopped anchovies to the pan, along with the butter and port. Heat gently, so the butter melts but doesn't bubble. Stir with a wooden spoon; the mixture will turn a milky brown colour. Keep stirring until the anchovies dissolve and you are left with a liquid. Roughly chop the remainder of the anchovies and add them to the pan to warm through. Pour the mixture into a ceramic dish and leave it to cool before putting it in the refrigerator to set.

Variation: grill a lamb chop for three minutes on each side until medium rare. Transfer to a serving plate and smear with the anchovy paste. Even anchovy evaders will like this.

CHORIZO AND SHALLOTS
IN CIDER VINEGAR

I first tasted this dish in Barcelona in a small tapas bar which didn't look particularly welcoming, but the aroma coming from the bar was so good I judged it worth trying.

SERVES 2

200g small chorizo sausages
10 shallots, peeled
40ml cider vinegar
handful flat-leaf parsley, chopped, to serve

Preheat the oven to 200°C/180°C fan/400°F/Gas mark 6. Place the chorizo sausages and whole shallots in an ovenproof dish with the cider vinegar and bake for 30 minutes. The juices from the sausages will intermingle with those from the cider vinegar to delicious effect. Sprinkle over the flat-leaf parsley and serve.

Variation: substitute regular pork sausages, plus a teaspoon of paprika and a couple of cloves of garlic, for the chorizo sausages.

ROAST FILLET OF BEEF WITH SHALLOTS IN A CREAMY MUSHROOM SAUCE

This is a great way of celebrating a good harvest of French shallots. I prefer to buy steak from the local butcher; it may be a bit more expensive than the supermarket, but it never disappoints. It's crucial to support local butchers; as well as offering great quality meat, they know exactly where their meat has come from and can offer endless ideas on the tastiest cuts and how to cook them.

SERVES 4

20ml olive oil,
  plus extra for drizzling
800g beef fillet
sprig thyme
12 shallots
4 cloves garlic
12 black peppercorns

50g unsalted butter
200g field mushrooms,
  thinly sliced
20ml balsamic vinegar
10ml brandy
100ml double cream
salt and pepper

Preheat the oven to 220°C/200°C fan/425°F/Gas mark 7. Pour the oil into a heavy-based, ovenproof frying pan and heat until it's searingly hot. Season the beef with salt and pepper and brown it all over. Remove the pan from the heat and add the thyme, shallots and garlic cloves in their skins, along with the peppercorns. Give the pan a good shake before transferring it to the oven for 25 minutes.

Carefully remove the hot frying pan from the oven, take out the beef and put it on a warm plate to rest. Return the frying pan to the hob, add half the butter, a drizzle of olive oil and the mushrooms and cook over a medium heat. When the mushrooms are lightly browned, pour in the balsamic vinegar and sizzle with the juices in the pan. Reduce the heat and stir in the brandy. Add the remaining butter, and when it has melted, slowly add the cream, making sure all the residues in the pan are mixed into the bubbling, velvety sauce.

Cut the steak into thick slices and serve two slices to each person. It is at its best rare on the inside and caramelised outside. Give the end pieces to anyone who prefers medium done steak. Ladle the mushroom, shallot and pepper sauce generously over the steak slices. The shallots will be caramelised on the outside, but soft and juicy on the inside. Serve with creamy mash and wilted spinach or steamed leeks.

Strawberries

Freshly picked ripe strawberries are the essence of a British summer. Eating as you pick is a rite of passage and a guilty pleasure. For me, strawberries are bite-sized memories. When I was little more than a toddler we had an elderly neighbour who had turned most of her back garden into a strawberry patch. On summer evenings, she generously shared enormous bowls of strawberries with us. There was also a lot of sugar and cream. These days, I more often accompany my scarlet jewels with Greek yoghurt, perhaps a grind of black pepper or a sprinkling of mint, though I believe that there is nothing better than Cornish clotted cream with strawberries.

Strawberries freeze well, but are slightly squishy when defrosted, so limited in their use. It's best to freeze them individually on trays before putting them in a freezer bag. Nothing beats a freshly picked strawberry though, so try to eat them when they are at their best.

STRAWBERRY AND CREAM MERINGUES

Fresh strawberries are an indulgence and what better way to indulge than with a sweet, crumbly meringue and thick cream. This dish isn't for every day, but worth looking forward to as a special treat.

SERVES 4

3 egg whites
1 teaspoon lemon juice, plus an extra squeeze
170g caster sugar
300g strawberries, halved

1 vanilla pod
250ml whipping cream, whipped
a few strands orange zest, finely chopped
pinch salt

Preheat the oven to 130°C/110°C fan/250°F/Gas mark ½. Put the egg whites, salt and lemon juice in a large bowl and whisk ferociously. Alternatively, you can use an electric mixer, as the egg whites do need a lot of whisking. When the whites stand up in peaks, beat in the sugar a little at a time. Again this will take a while if done by hand. The mixture will eventually look deliciously glossy and stand up well.

Cover a baking tray in non-stick baking paper and either spoon or pipe the meringues on to it: 10 centimetres in diameter is about the right size. Bake in the oven for about 1½ hours. A hint of colour is fine, but don't let them burn. Remove the meringues from the oven and allow to cool.

Put the strawberries in a bowl and sprinkle a few drops of lemon juice over them. Cut the vanilla pod in half and fold the seeds into the whipped cream along with the orange zest.

To serve, dollop a generous amount of cream onto the flat side of a meringue and then a little more. Pile as many strawberries as possible on top of the cream and eat straight away.

SALTED STRAWBERRIES

Nothing accentuates the sweetness of a strawberry more than salt.
This combination of caramel, strawberries and a hint of salt makes
the strawberries taste even sweeter, even more indulgent.

SERVES 4

100g soft brown sugar
20ml water
1 teaspoon salt flakes

100g unsalted butter
500g strawberries
100g plain chocolate, melted
(optional)

Put the sugar and water in a saucepan over a high heat until
the sugar dissolves. Reduce the temperature a little so the
syrup doesn't burn. Keep it just warm enough for the liquid
to reduce and turn a beautiful golden caramel colour. When
the syrup coats the back of a spoon, remove the pan from the
heat. Sprinkle in the salt and add the butter a lump at a time,
stirring as you go.

Lay the strawberries on a sheet of non-stick baking paper
and drizzle the salted caramel from a height, so that each
strawberry has a few lines of the sauce. Allow to cool in the
refrigerator. As an optional extra, drizzle melted chocolate
over the strawberries – the darker the better.

STRAWBERRY AND HONEY SMOOTHIE

In a really good season I freeze excess strawberries. They do tend to go a bit squishy, but that doesn't matter when you're making smoothies. In summer this drink is a refreshing, cool treat. In winter it's a luxury which reminds you of summer.

SERVES 2

200g strawberries, fresh or frozen
1 overripe banana
200ml milk
100g plain yoghurt
2 teaspoons clear honey

Put the strawberries, banana, milk and yoghurt in a blender and whizz. Pour the smoothie into a couple of tall glasses and stir in a spoonful or two of honey. If it's a hot day, add a couple of ice cubes.

Sweetcorn

I have discovered that badgers love sweetcorn and will happily chomp through three or four cobs a night while trampling the plants. So timing the harvest is crucial: knowing when the cobs are ready – succulent, ripe, swollen with rain and golden from the sun. I know that the longer I leave them the better they will become, but if I leave them too long I will end up with none. As soon as you pick sweetcorn cobs they start to lose flavour, so get them into the pot as quickly as you can. Sweetcorn is one crop that often tastes best when simply boiled in salted water and served with melted butter.

SWEETCORN FRITTERS WITH CHILLI AND LIME DRESSING

These fritters make a lovely light lunch. The natural sweetness of the corn brightens every mouthful. It's best to use cooked kernels, so you may need to boil a few cobs in advance, though I think this recipe is even worth opening a tin for.

SERVES 4

2 eggs, beaten
100ml milk
200g plain flour
1 teaspoon turmeric
1 teaspoon cumin seeds
300g sweetcorn kernels

10ml vegetable oil
juice 1 lime
30ml olive oil
2 teaspoons chilli flakes
pinch salt

In a small bowl, mix the eggs and milk. Put the flour in a large bowl, make a well in the centre and gradually mix in the liquid. Sprinkle in the turmeric, cumin seeds and sweetcorn and put to one side for 15 minutes.

Heat the vegetable oil in a non-stick frying pan over a high heat. When it is hot, spoon in the batter mixture, a spoonful at a time. Flatten each spoonful so it forms a pancake about 1cm thick. Cook for a couple of minutes on each side until golden.

Pour the lime juice into the olive oil and add the salt and chilli flakes. Stir well. Pour over the hot fritters and eat straight away.

CHICKEN AND SWEETCORN SOUP

I dislike wasting anything in the kitchen, so after we've devoured the meat from a roast chicken I usually simmer the bones for stock. When there are a few cobs of sweetcorn ready to be harvested, I always turn to this soup. It's fresh, heartening and packed with flavour.

SERVES 4

1 chicken carcass
2 litres water
4 cloves garlic, peeled
2 bay leaves
2 sweetcorn cobs,
    kernels removed
    (or 1 × 200g tin of kernels)

1 small red chilli,
    finely chopped
100g green leek leaves,
    cut into slivers
juice 1 lemon
2 eggs, beaten
pinch salt
crusty bread, to serve

Put the carcass in the biggest saucepan you have, breaking it into pieces to fit the pan. Add the water, a pinch of salt, the garlic and bay leaves, bring to the boil and simmer gently for a good hour – add an extra half hour if you have time.

Remove the chicken carcass and allow it to cool. Pick every morsel of chicken off the carcass and set to one side. Strain the remaining liquid, so you have a clear broth. Add the sweetcorn kernels to the broth with the chicken pieces, as well as the chilli and leek slivers. Simmer gently for 40 minutes, then turn off the heat. Add the lemon juice and stir, then trickle the beaten eggs into the soup, stirring gently as you go. Serve immediately with crusty bread.

Tomatoes

....

When a tomato is at its most perfect, I think you can almost taste the sunshine that ripened it. The flavour cannot be beaten. When it reaches ultimate ripeness it will almost fall from the plant into your hand – sweet, juicy, firm and bursting with colour.

I'd rather pick tomatoes a tad early than late, as they will redden even after they have been brought inside. I also believe that, unlike most produce, a tomato is best left for a day or two after picking. If I were a plant psychologist I'd suggest that they relax a bit. (I accept that's clearly nuts.) A freshly picked tomato often feels a bit taut and tense, and with a little time it softens and I'm convinced it becomes tastier too. Whatever you do, never put tomatoes in the refrigerator: that destroys their flavour. I enjoy small, yellow pear-shaped tomatoes and huge Italian Costoluto Fiorentinos, French Marmande and black cherry tomatoes. There are thousands of varieties and it's worth trying a wide selection.

TOMATO AND MOZZARELLA SALAD

It is often agonising waiting for the first tomatoes to ripen. Then the moment comes when there are just enough perfectly ripe ones for the first decent salad of the season. Harvesting is like selecting the cast for a play; a few beef, a couple of cherries, some red, some yellow, some with a French sensibility, others bursting with Italian flavour. The ensemble will be sure to perform when they meet the mozzarella.

SERVES 2

400g rested ripe tomatoes, halved
20g basil leaves, torn
120g ball mozzarella, torn into pieces

10ml lemon juice, plus zest
20ml extra-virgin olive oil
pinch coarse salt crystals and freshly ground white pepper
fresh bread, to serve

Put the tomatoes in a bowl and sprinkle with the salt and white pepper. Add the torn basil leaves and the mozzarella pieces. Pour over the lemon juice, zest and olive oil and serve with fresh bread or crackers for a memorable experience.

TOMATO SAUCE (HOME AND AWAY) WITH SPAGHETTI

As the summer progresses, you will have loads of ripe fruit which are perfect for making tomato sauce. This sauce really does sing, whether it's the smooth version I make at home or the less refined holiday one. Either way, with pasta and Parmesan, it is music to my ears.

SERVES 4–6

1kg ripe tomatoes, roughly chopped

20ml extra-virgin olive oil, plus extra to serve

1 large onion (about 250g), roughly chopped

4 cloves garlic, chopped

175ml red wine

30ml balsamic vinegar

20g basil leaves, torn

300ml water

300g spaghetti

pinch salt

Parmesan, to serve

Sprinkle the tomatoes with a generous pinch of salt. Heat the oil in a saucepan, add the onion and garlic and cook over a low heat until softened. Add the tomatoes and their juice. Cook slowly until the tomatoes start to break down. Pour in the red wine and balsamic vinegar and add half the basil leaves. Continue to cook the sauce gently for ten minutes.

Meanwhile cook the pasta: put the water in a large saucepan and bring to the boil, add the spaghetti and cook according to the packet instructions. At home I add the remaining basil leaves to the sauce, then whizz the mixture in a blender, adding water to get the desired consistency, and then sieve before serving. On holiday without electrical appliances, the coarseness is fine and you should just add the rest of the basil in the last few minutes. Serve on the spaghetti with a splosh of extra-virgin olive oil and a grating of Parmesan.

MEATBALLS WITH TOMATO SAUCE

I love making meatballs, especially with my son. It feels like a very Italian thing to do, heart-warming and rewarding, even though I'm not Italian. The breadcrumbs and Parmesan give these meatballs a light texture and the hint of anchovy provides a deep salty hit.

SERVES 4–6 (about 18–20 meatballs)

handful plain flour

70g fine breadcrumbs, made from 1 thick slice stale crusty bread

50g Parmesan, finely grated, plus extra to serve

2 medium onions, finely chopped

4 cloves garlic, finely chopped

750g beef mince

20g anchovy fillets, chopped

15g each sage, oregano and basil, finely chopped

1 large egg, beaten

500ml tomato sauce (see page 132)

freshly ground black pepper

cooked spaghetti drizzled with extra-virgin olive oil, to serve

---

Preheat the oven to 220°C/200°C fan/425°F/Gas mark 7. Sprinkle the flour on a board. Put the breadcrumbs into a large mixing bowl with the Parmesan. Add the onion and garlic, along with the mince and anchovies. Follow this with the sage, oregano and basil together with a good grind of black pepper and the egg. Mix everything together with your hands, then start rolling the meatballs. Golf-ball size is perfect, and as you finish each one, gently roll it in the flour to finish.

Place the meatballs in rows in a roasting tin and cook for ten minutes. Lower the temperature to 190°C/170°C fan/ 375°F/Gas mark 5 and pour over enough tomato sauce to come halfway up each meatball. Return the tin to the oven for a further 30 minutes, turning the meatballs halfway through. The flour coating helps to thicken the sauce, but if you feel it is too thick, add a few spoonfuls of water.

Five minutes before the end of the cooking time, grate Parmesan over the meatballs and then serve them hot from the oven with a bowl of spaghetti drizzled with extra-virgin olive oil.

ITALY ON TOAST

This incredibly simple recipe can be eaten at breakfast, lunch or any time in between. Use the sweetest tomatoes you have to hand, preferably on the vine.

SERVES 2

4 plump sweet tomatoes
10ml extra-virgin olive oil
10ml balsamic vinegar
1 sprig thyme
2 cloves garlic, unpeeled

4 thick slices ciabatta
200g mozzarella, sliced
a few basil leaves, torn
coarse sea salt and black
  pepper

Preheat the oven to 190°C/170°C fan/375°F/Gas mark 5. Put the tomatoes in an ovenproof dish with the olive oil, balsamic vinegar, thyme and garlic cloves. Season with salt and pepper and slow roast for about 40 minutes.

Remove the dish from the oven and carefully ease the vine from the tomatoes; try to keep their shape. Lightly toast the ciabatta slices. Squeeze the garlic onto the bread and spread it evenly. Cover the ciabatta slices with pieces of mozzarella and put them under a hot grill until the cheese starts to melt. Arrange the tomatoes on top and sprinkle with tiny pieces of torn basil, coarse sea salt and black pepper.

ROAST TOMATO SOUP WITH BASIL OIL

I tend to make this soup when I have quite a few soft and squidgy tomatoes. It freezes really well, and eaten on a cold winter's day it tastes and smells of sunshine.

SERVES 4–6

750g slightly overripe tomatoes, halved
20ml olive oil
20ml sherry vinegar
6 cloves garlic, unpeeled
2 teaspoons paprika
1 litre vegetable stock
salt and black pepper
crusty bread, to serve

for the basil oil
20g basil
20ml lemon juice
40ml extra-virgin olive oil
salt

Preheat the oven to 150°C/130°C fan/250°F/Gas mark 2. Lay the tomatoes cut side up in a roasting dish. Drizzle with the olive oil and sherry vinegar and sprinkle with salt and pepper. Add the garlic cloves and the paprika. Roast in the oven for an hour.

Remove the garlic and set it aside for the basil oil. Blitz everything else in the blender. Add about half the stock to the blender, then strain the liquid to remove skins, seeds and garlic skin. Push through as much of the tomato flesh as possible. Add more stock (how much depends on how thick you like soup), remembering that as you reheat the soup, it will reduce a little.

Squeeze the garlic you set aside into a food processor along with the other ingredients for the basil oil. Blend until smooth. Drizzle the basil oil over the hot soup and serve with crusty bread.

TOMATO CHUTNEY

Chutney season arrives when you realise that many of your tomatoes aren't likely to fully ripen. You can wrap them in newspaper or leave them on a windowsill, but sooner or later you will need to use them. Chutney is not a bad swansong at the end of summer and slightly firmer tomatoes are better here. I like this recipe so much that I'd be disappointed if I didn't end up with a bag of green tomatoes at the end of the summer. As you transform the hard green fruits into a viscous syrupy liquid, the aroma warms the kitchen. By the time you spoon the cooled chutney into small jars, you'll be thinking of Christmas, open fires, port and the cheese board that you will serve alongside this amazing chutney in a couple of months' time. This quantity should make enough for a generous jar for yourself, plus a couple of small jars to give as Christmas gifts.

MAKES 4 × 150ml JARS

600g green tomatoes, roughly chopped
1 large red onion, sliced
4 cloves garlic, roughly chopped
10ml olive oil
3 teaspoons chilli powder

250g soft brown sugar
300ml white wine vinegar
125g pitted dates, roughly chopped
juice 1 lime (optional)
3 tablespoons salt

Sprinkle the tomatoes with the salt and leave for at least an hour. Pour off any excess juice. Put the onions and garlic with the olive oil in a saucepan and soften over a medium heat for about five minutes. Lower the heat, add the chilli powder and sugar and give them a good stir before adding the tomatoes. Pour in the vinegar and stir to ensure the sugar dissolves. Bring the mixture to the boil, then reduce to a simmer and stir in the dates. Simmer for about 40 minutes; this is better judged by eye rather than a timer. Stir regularly as it simmers, to make sure that the thickening mixture does not catch and burn on the bottom of the pan.

By the time it is cooked, the tomatoes and onions will have softened to the point where they are unrecognisable and the liquid will have a hint of runniness, but be verging on a thick syrup. Add the lime juice at the end for an extra kick. Allow the chutney to cool and then spoon into sterilised jars.

It is now...

Inevitably, our summers are never long enough and they often seem to be over before they have really got going. Once the longest day's sun has set, it's a race to get all the work done in the garden before autumn blows in. Weeds flower and seed, staking a claim on next year's beds. Food is abundant, but as the produce is harvested, there is less and less to plant in its place. Woody stems need to be cut back and soil turned. Some beds are covered with tarpaulin and heavy bricks put in place to stop it blowing away when there are gales.

As the last batches of courgettes are picked, nearby squashes and pumpkins give a glimmer of colour, the sign of a plentiful autumn to come. By now, the freezer is full of fruit and meals that will warm and satisfy through the darker evenings. As the sunflowers bow, then droop, and apples fall from the trees, it's clear that summer is over.

Summer feeds me well and the flavours and variety of the season's foods are breathtaking. They will be missed, like the sun. At this time of year, the line between joy and sadness is fine: suddenly all that is left on the plot are cabbages and roots and it's hard to get excited by turnips, kale and parsnips. But the September evening sun is rare and golden and its glow makes the crops that remain look more enticing. The potatoes and onions will keep, but now is the perfect time to devour the final tomatoes. The spinach still has a few younger leaves which will go in a salad and the wild rocket and mizuna are hanging on in the greenhouse, before I clear it for autumn.

Batten down the hatches.

Autumn

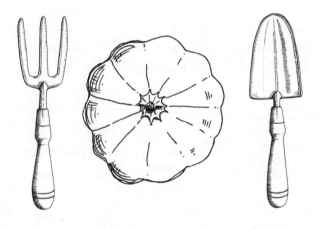

What to plant and harvest in autumn

Sow

early carrots

Plant

broad beans

spring cabbages

fruit trees

garlic

raspberry canes

rhubarb crowns

strawberry plants

shallots

Harvest

apples

blackberries

celery

herbs

Jerusalem artichokes

mushrooms

onions

pears

potatoes

pumpkins

squash

AUTUMN RECIPES

Apples and pears

Stilton, pear and red onion tart

*Roast belly of pork
with black pudding, apples and roast veg*

Baked apples with Calvados syrup

Pear, Gorgonzola and chicory salad

Pears in red wine

Rustic ravioli

Blackberries

Autumn fruit surprise

Rice pudding and jam

Celery

Celery, apple, beetroot and ginger salad

Chowder

Lamb shanks

Jerusalem artichokes

Cream of Jerusalem artichoke soup with truffle oil

Jerusalem crisps

Slow roast pork shoulder
with a potato and Jerusalem artichoke mattress

Mushrooms

Walnut and Stilton stuffed mushrooms

Chicken and mushrooms in red wine

Autumn en croute with creamed spinach

Onions

Red onion jam

White onion marmalade

Piccalilli with ham on the side

Onion soup with shallot and cheese croutons

Potatoes (maincrop)

Rib-eye steak with thick chips

Almost perfect roasties

Sausages and mash with thick red onion gravy

'Eel taps 'n' eggs

Tapas (aka Tatty tapas)

Rosemary

Hake with capers in a lemon and rosemary sauce
Rosemary roast potatoes with garlic, chorizo and mozzarella

Squash and pumpkins

Butternut squash soup
Frighteningly good pumpkin stew
Warm goat's cheese, squash and red onion salad
Butternut squash, fennel and red pepper with couscous
Baked custard white squash with leeks, garlic and Parmesan
Spaghetti squash Italiano
Lamb neck fillets with squash and potatoes

In praise of the ever darkening days...

Just as spring's arrival is sudden, the immediacy of autumn can be dramatic. Starkness often arrives overnight. When the autumn leaves begin to swirl, it's a good indicator that the salad days of summer are well and truly over. Whilst I appreciate that this sounds depressingly like a euphemism for middle age (or at least the start of a mid-life crisis), I make no apology. If ever there is a time for a gardener to experience severe mood swings, it's now.

September's harvest is a grow-your-own equivalent of the FA cup final: I have worked tirelessly for months and made it through all the trials and tribulations that nature could throw at me. Despite frosts, floods, drought, slugs, blight and aphids, I now have my hands on the ultimate prize: a wheelbarrow groaning with produce; the envy of my neighbours.

Cruelly, no sooner have I pulled the last of my onions, early leeks and beetroot; plucked the juiciest apples from the tree and dug the last few orderly rows of maincrop potatoes; than I am left with mud. The bare patches of earth, where previously an oasis of veg once flourished, are now merely home to a few persistent weeds and even they look a bit shell-shocked by the seasonal change. Often the best thing to do is just to cover the beds until the urge to dig them overcomes the mini depression that marks the end of the growing season. To make matters worse, the summer clock will soon shift, the days get dramatically shorter and as autumn stamps its feet and begins to breathe cold air, the only crops with any inclination to grow seem to belong to the cabbage family.

On the surface, autumn is hardly something to look forward to. My gloom is lifted by the appreciation of my new autumnal best friends. Soon it will be time for the pumpkins to take centre stage. These little parcels of sunshine and hope lie on the black earth soaking up every last ray. When they are cooked they radiate all that sunshine back from the plate. Unfortunately they are not quite ready (the traditionalist in me waits for Halloween). The fruit will soon rain down from the trees to sweeten the darkest of days and my stray potatoes will keep me warm and nourished in the most delightful ways. The al fresco life may no longer be possible – or at least practical – but once I get over that and start to enjoy what the season has to offer, I discover a whole new lease of culinary life.

The shed heaves with the autumn harvest. With renewed vigour and determination, I roll up my sleeves and start cooking. Within days, chutneys and pickles line the kitchen. Soups, pies and curries fill the freezer. It's a case of 'use it or lose it' and after working so hard to raise all this produce, no gardener wants to give up on it. Consequently autumn is one of my busiest times in the kitchen.

It's not long before the shock of autumn gives way to its charm. As the season progresses, there are often days when the quality of light, the troubled grey skies, the cool gasp of the wind and the palette of maturity are as attractive as spring's youthfulness.

On the plate, things change too. Autumnal veg is robust, so dishes evolve and become more substantial, heartier and increasingly comforting. Now, less tender cuts of meat don't feel like too much bother. Cooking just takes a little longer. Good job then, that the nights are getting colder and darker. The temptation to walk around the plot certainly wanes, as the rain lashes and panes of glass blow out of the greenhouse. From here on, however dark it is outside, there's always a warm glow in the kitchen (especially if red wine is factored in).

So I guess if I ever had a therapist, I would have to admit that vegetables, one way or another, get me through the darkening days. Now I've said it, I feel better already.

Autumn, in the end, cheers me and nourishes me.

Apples and pears

Apple and pear trees are essential to the plot. Year after year they groan with fruit and ask for very little in return. Julie, who has the plot beside me, runs a community orchard and grows a fantastic range of apples and pears, including many rare varieties. A couple of times a year, Julie and her fellow volunteers have an open day in the orchard, with cider and juice tasting, and make fabulous apple and pear cakes and pies. This is a marker for me (like the equinox), a little reminder that for a few weeks I shall be making the most of some of our country's most reliable fruit.

The trick with apples is getting to the windfalls before the slugs. This does require a daily patrol – and even then it's rare to find uninhabited fruits. Culinary invention is essential.

Pears are a challenge too. They remain hard and impenetrable for weeks. The trouble is, they yearn to be picked long before they are ready. They practically jump out of the trees – touch them even gently and they will fall. It takes a lot to ripen a pear and what they need is usually in short supply. So any pear grower will tell you that they harvest them carefully and painstakingly store the fruit in boxes, not touching, in a place which is not too dark, and does not get too much sun. It's a laborious business and they need to be checked daily for signs of ripeness. What usually happens is that they all ripen at the same time, so a pear fest is inevitable. It's not so bad.

STILTON, PEAR AND RED ONION TART

This is a bit flash. Although it's pretty simple, with a bit of care in presentation it can make a really bold statement. It's a sweet, salty, tangy delight, which is accentuated by a simple leaf salad. Of course it also looks amazing – always important (or is that just the TV producer in me?). This is a 'wow' dish that will be polished off pretty quickly.

SERVES 4 (OR A GREEDY 2)

20g Demerara sugar
20g unsalted butter
20ml balsamic vinegar
4 smallish red onions,
   cut into 1cm rings

4 pears, cut into 1cm slices
flour, for rolling out pastry
375g ready-made puff pastry
   (1 packet)
100g Stilton

Preheat the oven to 200°C/180°C fan/400°F/Gas mark 6. Put an ovenproof non-stick frying pan over a medium heat and heat the sugar until it caramelises. Add the butter and vinegar to make a thick caramel that gloops over the whole pan base. Reduce gently if you have more than that, then remove from the heat.

Arrange the onions and pears in the pan. I favour a geometric swirl of pear crescents radiating out from the centre of the pan, with a regiment of onions circling the edge. If you have any pear or onion slices left, use them to fill holes.

On a floured surface, roll out the pastry and trim it so it is a little larger than the frying pan. Place the pastry over the pan so it tightly blankets the pear and onion and tuck it in. Cook in the oven for 30 minutes, until the pastry is puffed and golden.

Turn the tart pastry-side down onto a serving plate, sprinkle with crumbs of Stilton and flash under a hot grill for a minute, so the cheese starts to melt.

ROAST BELLY OF PORK WITH BLACK PUDDING, APPLES AND ROAST VEG

This is a meal for a dark night. I mean dark in the visual sense, but it will also cheer you up with its warming and deep flavours, so it's good comfort food too: a dish to make you look forward to autumn.

SERVES 4–6

2kg boned pork belly, skin lightly scored

500ml dry cider

3 teaspoons fennel seeds, crushed

20g soft brown sugar

4 apples, peeled and quartered

2 red onions, peeled and quartered

4 carrots, cut into 5cm chunks

4 cloves garlic, chopped

250g black pudding, cut into 3cm rings

3 teaspoons coarse sea salt

Put the pork in a shallow dish and pour over the cider. Marinate for a couple of hours or more; overnight if you have time.

Preheat the oven to 220°C/200°C fan/425°F/Gas mark 7. Remove the pork from the marinade, setting the cider to one side. Pat the skin dry and put the pork on a wire tray above a dish for half an hour to allow the skin to fully dry. This will help make the crackling crisp, and collect any excess cider. Rub two teaspoons of the fennel seeds and the sea salt into the pork skin, transfer the meat on the wire tray to a roasting tin and put it in the hot oven for 20 minutes.

Meanwhile, simmer the cider marinade in a saucepan, skimming off the impurities as they rise to the surface. Add a further teaspoon of fennel seeds and the soft brown sugar. Once the sugar dissolves, you will have a clear brown liquid. Reduce this slowly for ten minutes, then turn off the heat. Baste the pork with the cider sauce and reduce the oven temperature to 170°C/150°C fan/325°F/Gas mark 3. Roast for a further hour, basting every ten minutes or so.

Remove the pork from the oven and lift the meat on the

wire rack out of the roasting tin. Put the apples, onions, carrots and garlic into the roasting tin and rest the pork on top. Baste with a couple more spoonfuls of cider syrup and pop back into the oven for a further 40 minutes.

Add the black pudding rings to the roasting tin for the final 15 minutes or so of cooking. Remove the pork from the oven and set it to one side to rest. Transfer the vegetables and mushy apples to a warm serving bowl. Deglaze the roasting tray with the remaining cider sauce and reduce by half. Strain.

Put a generous slice of pork belly with a ring of black pudding and a large dollop of apple on each plate. Pour over the gravy and serve with the roasted veg and mashed or roast potatoes.

BAKED APPLES WITH CALVADOS SYRUP

*I remember my mum making this for me and my grandad, Fred,
when I was a child (the baked apple – there was no Calvados syrup).
Memories tell me that it was the most magical thing I had ever tasted.
I can still recall the sweet smell filling the house and the anticipation
I felt waiting for the apples to be brought to the table, adorned with
cream. As I tucked in to my first sticky sweet mouthful I must have
looked up, because my grandad, normally a man who reflected his
Victorian childhood, smiled back – a rare occurrence. Clearly, he too
appreciated the simple delights of caramelised apple. I think, for a
moment, we bonded.*

SERVES 4

50g sultanas
50ml Calvados
4 medium cooking apples,
   cored
200g light brown sugar

few drops lemon juice
25g unsalted butter
100ml water
1 cinnamon stick
clotted cream, to serve

Soak the sultanas in the Calvados for a good hour, then
drain and put the Calvados to one side. Preheat the oven to
170°C/150°C fan/325°F/Gas mark 3. Fill the centre of each
apple with sugar (keeping 20g to one side for the syrup),
the sultanas and a drop or two of lemon juice. Pack them in
tightly and plug the gap with a knob of butter. Bake the apples
in the oven, on a baking tray, for around 20–30 minutes,
until soft.

For the syrup, dissolve the remaining sugar in the water, add
the cinnamon stick and reduce. As the liquid turns golden and
begins to caramelise, add the Calvados and stir for a few more
minutes, until the alcohol evaporates. Remove from the heat.
Drizzle the syrup over the hot apples and serve immediately
with thick clotted cream for a sweet, sensational dessert.

PEAR, GORGONZOLA AND CHICORY SALAD

Sweet pears, salty Gorgonzola, slightly bitter chicory and crunchy celery make up this refreshing salad. The beauty is in the simplicity. I guess this isn't really cooking; it's actually assembling. The pears need to be at the peak of ripeness and that can mean a bit of a waiting game. With such a simple combination of ingredients, it's worth making an effort with the presentation. Keep the chicory leaves whole, the pear slices thin and the celery pieces the same length as the pears. The combination of textures and flavours is spectacular.

SERVES 4

**2 large ripe pears,
   peeled and thinly sliced**
250g chicory leaves
**3 sticks celery, cut to the same
   length as the chicory leaves**
**150g Gorgonzola,
   cut into small pieces**
**20g chopped walnuts
   (optional)**

for the dressing
50ml sherry vinegar
200ml olive oil
freshly ground black pepper

Arrange the pear slices, chicory and celery in a serving dish. Nestle the Gorgonzola pieces amid the greenery. Mix the vinegar and olive oil to make the dressing, add a grind or two of black pepper and lightly dress the salad. Sometimes I add a sprinkling of chopped walnuts.

PEARS IN RED WINE

The great joy of this dish from a grower's point of view is that the pears don't need to be perfectly ripe – in fact a tad on the firm side is preferable. This is a visually impressive and totally delicious dessert best made a day in advance for maximum flavour.

SERVES 6

6 medium pears, peeled, but with stalks in place
200ml red wine (the darker the better)
50g light brown sugar
2 tablespoons clear honey

6 cloves
6 peppercorns
1 cinnamon stick
zest 1 orange
150g mascarpone, to serve

Use a saucepan in which the pears can stand upright. Put the red wine in the saucepan over a gentle heat and dissolve the sugar and honey in it. The pears need to stand up to their necks in liquid, so top up the saucepan with a little water if needed. Add all the other ingredients and bring to a boil, simmering for a good 15 minutes until the pears soften. Put everything into an airtight container and store in the refrigerator for 24 hours.

Put a pear on each serving plate and heat the liquid in a saucepan over a medium heat until it has reduced by half. Pour the syrup over the pears and serve with a spoonful of mascarpone on each plate.

RUSTIC RAVIOLI

I once filmed in a remote Tuscan cookery school for a week. The students made pasta every day, which didn't make for riveting television, but I learned how simple, satisfying and delicious pasta is, when made fresh. Choosing the right flour for pasta is partly an art, partly science and partly a matter of personal taste. Broadly, the stronger the flour, the more glutinous it will be and the fewer eggs you will need to hold it together. Eggs make the pasta richer (and in my view tastier) but if you only have strong plain flour in the cupboard when the pasta urge arrives, leave out the additional egg yolks, add a little water for consistency and all will be fine. If I were Italian, or had listened more carefully at the cookery school, I might tell you a different story.

Making pasta is essentially the same process as mixing cement by hand. I say this merely as a visual aid, as I accept that mixing cement isn't everybody's thing. I'm sure if I ever wrote a book about DIY I would struggle to convince would-be builders that an understanding of making pasta from scratch would help with the construction of a patio. Once the pasta dough is mixed and kneaded, a pasta machine will allow you to roll very thin sheets of pasta, which are ideal, but it's perfectly possible to use a large rolling pin instead.

It's important that the sauce you serve with the ravioli doesn't overpower the filling: it should complement and enhance the flavours rather than detract from them. Here the pear and ricotta are married perfectly with a creamy walnut sauce. Serving home-made ravioli to a bunch of mates is a pretty impressive act. You will get top culinary cred for this, although it really is a simple dish.

for the pasta
300g '00' flour
2 eggs, plus 2 yolks
30ml extra-virgin olive oil
1 teaspoon salt, plus extra for the pasta water

for the filling
2 firm pears, peeled, cored and cut into bite-sized pieces
100ml port
30g soft brown sugar

100g ricotta
for the sauce
100ml double cream
20g walnuts, lightly toasted and chopped
10ml walnut oil
6 sage leaves, finely chopped

On a large, clean work surface, make a heap of the flour and create a well in the top. Add the eggs, yolks, olive oil and salt. Mix with a fork and gradually combine the flour with the other ingredients. Once the flour is combined, begin to knead the pasta: 15 minutes is ideal. You will begin to feel it taking on more elasticity with every pounding. Rest the pasta under a damp tea towel for a while (perhaps long enough for a glass of wine and a sit down).

When rolling by hand, sprinkle some flour on the table and divide the pasta dough into quarters. You need to roll it as thin as possible, so it's better to do this in smaller quantities. Cut pasta circles using an upturned glass about 15cm in diameter. The circles should be bigger than you think they need to be, to allow for plenty of filling and a decent edge to seal together. Squares and rectangles work just as well.

For the filling, put the pear pieces in a saucepan with the port and sugar and simmer gently for 10–15 minutes. You need to reduce most of the liquid, leaving just a sticky coating, yet ensure that the pear chunks still have shape. As the mixture thickens and caramelises during the last few minutes, it's vital that it doesn't burn, so don't rush it. Allow to cool.

Put a teaspoon of ricotta and a chunk of pear on half of each pasta circle, leaving about a centimetre around the edge. Fold the pasta over the filling and seal, using a little water to moisten the edges. Make sure that each parcel is carefully sealed, otherwise the filling will escape. Fill your largest saucepan with water, add salt and bring it to the boil. Carefully put the ravioli in and simmer for 2–3 minutes before draining.

For the sauce, gently warm the cream, add the walnuts and the oil and then the sage. Serve it lightly drizzled over the ravioli – you don't need a great deal.

Variation: Gorgonzola works brilliantly with pear too, though you will need to use less. Once you have mastered the basics, experiment with different filling combinations. Porcini mushroom and cream cheese is a favourite, served with a light tomato sauce.

Blackberries

I have rogue blackberry bushes at either end of the plot. Throughout the year they are a menace: tearing clothes and scratching skin. Pruning essentially involves hacking off any branches that get in my way. So it's fair to say they are not the most lovingly tended plants on the allotment. Fickle as I am, in the autumn, as soon as there is a glimpse of some food, they are welcome. Best friends, even. I think at one time these bushes were from cultivated stock, rather than wild plants, as the berries are huge, succulent and delicious. Of course I still raid the occasional wild blackberry bush too, but they seem increasingly hard to find and the fruit is often very small and sparse in comparison to those grown on the plot. It goes without saying that all the best fruit grows in unreachable places. I wonder if there was a time that these cultivated bushes were under control and regimented; they have certainly lost any sense of discipline now. Still they feed the birds heartily for a few months and given that I didn't plant them, I am always grateful for my free lunch.

AUTUMN FRUIT SURPRISE

There are often days when dishes come together from necessity. This recipe came about on one such day. I had a few forgotten sticks of rhubarb knocking around and a pile of pears that weren't yet soft enough to eat. I quickly picked a bowl of blackberries and took the last fig from the tree. I had some leftover ends of puff pastry in the refrigerator and a hungry son with a sweet tooth. If you find yourself with pastry and almost any fruit to hand, give this a go. All sorts of things can happen during the cooking: the juice from the blackberries might explode in the pastry, or the pears caramelise, and the cooked fruit nestles into the rising puff pastry like a teenager in a duvet. Every bite is a delight and you will never get the same mouthful twice.

SERVES 4

320g puff pastry
flour, for rolling out
500g fruit, such as rhubarb, pears, blackberries, figs,
   autumn raspberries, apples, peeled and sliced as needed
50g caster sugar
20g icing sugar, to serve

Preheat the oven to 200°C/180°C fan/400°F/Gas mark 6. Roll out the pastry on a floured surface and cut it into random shapes, about the size of your palm. Place on a non-stick baking tray. Arrange a selection of fruit in the centre of each, making sure you leave a 2cm border around the edge. Score gently around the edge of the pastry with the back of a knife. Sprinkle the fruit with caster sugar and bake the pastries for 20–25 minutes. Sprinkle with icing sugar to serve. Nice with custard or cream.

RICE PUDDING AND JAM

I'm not a fan of the skin on rice pudding. I think it's because it's called 'skin': instantly unappealing. If the golden-brown topping were christened 'a sweet blanket' instead, I might be more tempted to cook this in the oven. I prefer to take a risotto-style approach, which makes the pudding creamy, filling and delightful, while the jam is sweet, sticky and sensational.

SERVES 4

for the rice pudding
30g unsalted butter
50g caster sugar
160g Arborio rice
750ml milk
300ml double cream
1 vanilla pod
salt

for the jam
50g sugar
150ml water
150g blackberries
1 apple, peeled and diced

Melt the butter in a saucepan over a gentle heat, then dissolve the sugar in it and coat the rice, stirring for a few minutes. Add the milk and cream. Stir well and bring to a simmer. Split the vanilla pod lengthways, scrape out the seeds and add both to the pan with a pinch of salt. Reduce the heat to very low, cover and allow to bubble away quietly for about an hour with a good stir every ten minutes or so; gloopy is the aim.

For the jam, put the sugar and water in a small saucepan and heat until the sugar dissolves, then add the blackberries and the apple. Simmer until the apples and blackberries are soft and most of the liquid has reduced. Serve with the creamy rice pudding (in the middle, or on a separate dish if you are posh).

Celery

....

Until I grew it myself, I always considered celery to be a spring or early summer salad crop. I never really appreciated it much; it was one of those things I picked up in the supermarket from time to time and left to grow limp in the refrigerator. Celery is a tricky customer to grow – it needs regular watering, weeding and earthing up. The celery I do manage to grow has fantastic flavour and over the past few years I have become more and more fond and respectful of it. Although it can be harvested in August, I increasingly find myself using it as an autumn crop. For that reason I rely on it less as a stick to eat in salad and much more as an ingredient to bring depth to other dishes. So despite being a high maintenance crop, it is a modest and hardworking ingredient in the kitchen. I use the stems in stews, casseroles and sauces and the leaves can replace parsley. The very young leaves hardly need cooking at all.

CELERY, APPLE, BEETROOT AND GINGER SALAD

Randomly shaped pieces of apple are ideal for this salad; they help to keep it interesting – perfect if you have a batch of windfall fruit. The celery, ginger and beetroot combine with the juicy sweet apple to make this salad vibrant, virtuous and full of vitality. It will brighten any autumn lunchbox, offering crunch, warmth and variety in every mouthful.

SERVES 4

3 apples, chopped into thumb-sized pieces

2–3 sticks celery, chopped into thumb-sized pieces

1 medium beetroot, grated

2cm piece ginger, peeled and grated

20ml lemon juice

2 teaspoons cumin seeds

20ml extra-virgin olive oil

1 tablespoon harissa

150g plain yoghurt

Put the apple and celery pieces in a mixing bowl. Add the beetroot and ginger with the lemon juice. Sprinkle in the cumin seeds and stir the mixture so the lemon juice coats everything. In a separate bowl, mix the oil, harissa and yoghurt. Drizzle over the salad.

CHOWDER

I believe there's only so much celery a person can eat raw before being driven to despair. Thankfully it is a powerful ingredient when cooked; it may lose a little distinctiveness, but the depth and flavour it adds to dishes make it well worth growing.

This creamy, indulgent fish stew is perfect for an autumn evening and the celery adds both flavour and texture. It's the recipe to make when the fishmonger has special offers, as most fish – apart from oily types such as mackerel – are perfect for it. I prefer to use floury potatoes such as Maris Piper or Desiree so they start to break down in the dish.

SERVES 4–6

500g floury potatoes, peeled
6 shallots, finely chopped
10ml olive oil
50g unsalted butter
200ml white wine
4 anchovies, chopped
2 leeks, sliced into
 finger-width pieces
3 sticks celery, sliced into
 finger-width pieces
750ml vegetable stock

3 teaspoons finely chopped
 tarragon
1 tablespoon Dijon mustard
400g meaty white fish,
 cut into large chunks
200g smoked undyed haddock,
 cut into large chunks
150g raw king prawns, shelled
100ml single cream
salt
crème fraîche, to serve

Boil the potatoes in salted water for 8–10 minutes to remove some of the starch. Don't cook them fully at this stage. Drain, cool and dice into bite-sized chunks.

Heat a saucepan and sauté the shallots gently in the oil and butter. As they start to soften, add the white wine and reduce by about half. Stir the anchovies into the pan, then add the leek, celery and potatoes. Pour in the stock and simmer for about ten minutes.

Add most of the tarragon (keeping a little for decoration) and the mustard. Stir well and then add the fish and the prawns. Simmer gently for a further ten minutes so the fish cooks through. Turn off the heat and stir in the cream. Serve immediately, with a blob of crème fraiche and a sprinkling of tarragon in each bowl.

LAMB SHANKS

This is a great October Saturday dish. It needs a long cooking time and after a busy week it's nice to batten down the hatches and unwind with a bit of a cooking fest. This dish fills the kitchen with marvellous aromas for hours, so by the time it hits the plate I'm more than ready for it. Eaten in a warm kitchen with a glass of red wine and the footie on the radio, it's perfect.

SERVES 4

4 lamb shanks (300–350g each)
plain flour, for dusting
6 cloves garlic, halved, plus 2 whole cloves
20ml olive oil
500ml red wine
400g carrots, roughly chopped
3 sticks celery, roughly chopped, plus leaves
2 large onions, roughly chopped
large sprig woody rosemary
large sprig lavender
1 bay leaf
250ml vegetable stock
10ml balsamic vinegar
salt and black pepper

Preheat the oven to 190°C/170°C fan/375°F/Gas mark 5. Season the shanks with salt and pepper and a dusting of flour. Make a couple of incisions in each shank and poke half a clove of garlic as far as you can into each slot. Heat the oil in a heavy frying pan and sear the lamb on all sides before transferring it to an ovenproof dish.

Deglaze the pan with the red wine, then pour it over the lamb. Pack the carrots, celery and onion around the meat and add the rosemary and lavender sprigs. Pop in the bay leaf and a couple more cloves of garlic, before adding the stock. Cover and cook in the oven for about 3½ hours.

Before serving, take the shanks out of the dish and put them in a warm place to rest for ten minutes while you reduce the gravy a little. Fish out the rosemary and lavender sprigs and add a splash of balsamic vinegar. Roast artichokes and braised cabbage complement this dish wonderfully.

Jerusalem artichokes

At first sight, Jerusalem artichokes resemble some kind of alien creature – maybe we should heed that first instinct; perhaps they are warning us not to eat them.

Many seasoned gardeners will tell you that they curse the day they planted these weird-looking tubers. They have amazing foliage, beautiful flowers and produce an abundant crop, but the inconvenient truth is that once you have planted them, you will never be without them – they are the vegetable world's repeat offenders, no less. No matter how many times I convince myself that every last tuber and root has been removed from the ground, they just keep coming back. Innocent little green shoots pop out of the ground first, then, within weeks they are towering above everything and proclaiming their belligerence. You can almost sense the overwhelming smugness of your neighbours as they knowingly smile at the yellow flowers gracefully swaying in the wind. Wind is, after all, their final gift.

Despite their weed-like tendencies, I've noticed the cost of these tubers spiralling in the shops recently. Somebody must be on to a good thing. My tip for anyone contemplating growing the odd tuber or two in the garden or veg patch is to plant them in an old dustbin or bath. That way you will contain their enthusiasm but can still relish the roasties, not to mention the soup...

CREAM OF JERUSALEM ARTICHOKE SOUP WITH TRUFFLE OIL

This has a luxurious taste. The velvety texture of the soup and the depth of flavour of the truffle oil elevates the dish to special occasion status. Of course if you grow artichokes you can have it as often as you like. Peeling the artichokes can be time-consuming, as they are random in shape, to say the least. I have tried boiling them in their skins and removing the jackets later, but it's almost as much of a palaver as peeling them, so just put on the radio and peel, I say.

SERVES 4

20g unsalted butter
10ml olive oil
1 onion, chopped
2 cloves garlic, chopped
juice 1 lemon
750g (8 large) Jerusalem artichokes, peeled and chopped into thumb-size chunks

1 bay leaf
600ml chicken stock
150ml double cream
salt and black pepper
truffle oil, to serve

Melt the butter in a large, heavy-based saucepan, add the oil and soften the onion for a few minutes. Add the garlic and heat gently for another couple of minutes. Pour in the lemon juice and reduce the liquid until it almost disappears. Add the artichokes, bay leaf and stock and bring gently to the boil. Simmer for 20 minutes, until the artichokes have softened.

Pour the soup into a blender and whizz until smooth before returning it to the pan. Add the cream, salt and pepper and stir. Serve piping hot with a drizzle of truffle oil, if you have some: it really complements the flavour of the artichokes.

Variation: carnivores can add a sprinkling of crisp streaky bacon slivers to garnish.

JERUSALEM CRISPS

It doesn't matter how many you make of these, they will all disappear. Fatter artichokes are best for this. You can use a mandoline to cut the paper-thin slices you need, but a sharp knife, keen eye and steady hand also does the job – eventually.

SERVES 4–6

500g Jerusalem artichokes, peeled and thinly sliced
20ml rapeseed oil
salt

Pour the oil into a heavy-based frying pan and heat until hot, then carefully drop in the artichoke slices, a batch at a time. Add more oil if needed. When the slices are crisp, place on kitchen paper till cool. The crisps are perfectly delicious with a generous sprinkling of salt. The best ones are crisp on the outside and chewy in the centre.

Variation: finely chopped flat-leaf parsley or a sprinkle of paprika make a healthier alternative to salt.

SLOW ROAST PORK SHOULDER ON A POTATO AND JERUSALEM ARTICHOKE MATTRESS

I'm at home with most culinary terms, yet I'm always amused and surprised by the elaborate descriptions given to dishes. I'm just about happy with French-inspired names such as 'jus', but I draw the line at the ridiculous. I was once served a 'rendezvous of vegetables', which turned out to be peas, carrots and sweetcorn. The quality of the eatery was such that the aforementioned veg must have arranged their meeting in a freezer bag. They certainly weren't thrown together by a chance encounter en route from the garden. However, given the soft springiness of the artichokes and potatoes in this dish, 'mattress' feels appropriate. After its long cook, the pork pulls apart effortlessly, while the potato mattress boasts a crisp top, with deep, soft layers that melt in the mouth.

SERVES 6

- 1.5kg piece pork shoulder, crackling scored at finger-width intervals
- 1.5kg potatoes, ideally King Edwards, peeled and thinly sliced
- 2 onions, thinly sliced
- 1kg Jerusalem artichokes, thinly sliced
- 1.5 litres chicken stock
- salt
- peas, to serve

Preheat the oven to 220°C/200°C fan/425°F/Gas mark 7. Pour a kettleful of boiling water over the joint and then pat the fat dry. Sprinkle with salt and rub it into the cracks.

Put the pork in a roasting dish with high sides and pop into the oven for 20–25 minutes until the crackling has crisped. Remove from the oven and reduce the temperature to 170°C/150°C fan/325°F/Gas mark 3. Take the pork out of the roasting dish and put to one side. Put alternate layers of potatoes, onions and artichokes into the roasting dish, being careful not to splash the hot pork fat. Create a mattress about 8–10 centimetres high. Pour in the stock and nestle the pork on top. Return to the oven for about four hours.

From time to time, move the joint to a different spot on the mattress. If you make the bed flat the slow drizzle of fat from the pork keeps the top level of the potatoes moist. If the potatoes crisp too quickly, cover the exposed areas with foil.

Allow the pork to rest before serving. If the crackling isn't crisp enough, carefully cut it off and flash under the grill for a few minutes. Serve with peas or, if you are feeling sophisticated, a medley, rendezvous or flashmob of seasonal veg: I like a liaison of leeks and carrots, but that's just the romantic in me.

Mushrooms

Nothing tastes better than free food and I find that foraging for a few mushrooms is well worth the effort. I get up earlier than I'd like, drive out to the countryside, traipse through the fields and pick the biggest dew-covered field mushrooms I can find. It's naturally fulfilling: if you are in any doubt, just try it. (For the purposes of my legislative freedom, I must add that you should only drive if you are over 17, haven't been drinking the night before and have the appropriate driving licence, insurance and road tax. Don't trespass and do check with an expert that what you're picking is a field mushroom and not something that's either going to kill you or send you into a hallucinogenic state for a long period.)

The long arm of the law aside, if you pick your own mushrooms you will appreciate this simple fungus more than you can imagine. In fact, you will hunger for the flavour of a freshly picked crop. Be sure to have some for breakfast when you return home.

WALNUT AND STILTON STUFFED MUSHROOMS

This simple dish – suitable for breakfast, lunch or dinner – is a wonderful marriage of intense flavours. The mushrooms ooze their dark juices into the molten, gooey Stilton and the nuts add texture and depth. It's incredibly filling, but you will want more anyway. If ever there was a reason to feel good about a British autumn, it's this.

SERVES 4

4 field mushrooms
2 teaspoons ground ginger
2 teaspoons chilli powder
2 cloves garlic, finely chopped
80g breadcrumbs

60g cream cheese
60g Stilton
60g walnuts, chopped
20ml olive oil
spinach or rocket leaves, to serve

Preheat the oven to 200°C/180°C fan/400°F/Gas mark 6. Remove the stalks from the mushrooms and a little of the flesh from inside the cups. Chop the flesh finely and put in a mixing bowl with all the other ingredients. Blend together with a wooden spoon to form a textured paste and spoon this back into the mushroom cups. Press down as firmly as you can. You will end up with quite a mound of filling.

Put the mushrooms in an ovenproof dish and bake for half an hour. The filling will melt and bubble, brown and ooze – don't worry about it. Serve with spinach or rocket leaves.

CHICKEN AND MUSHROOMS IN RED WINE

This recipe has a nod to coq au vin. It has immense flavour and is satisfying not only to eat but also to make.

SERVES 4–6

10ml olive oil
30g unsalted butter
6 chicken thighs
150g pancetta, cubed
4 cloves garlic,
   roughly chopped
10 shallots, left whole

200g mushrooms, quartered
1 tablespoon plain flour
500ml red wine
500ml chicken stock
2 bay leaves
20g flat-leaf parsley, chopped,
   to serve

Heat a wide, deep, saucepan (which has a lid) and add the oil and butter. When they sizzle, add the chicken thighs and cover the pan. Cook the chicken pieces for about five minutes on each side, until browned. Remove them and put to one side.

Put the pancetta in the saucepan with the garlic and shallots. Cook over a gentle heat for about five minutes. Add the mushrooms and cook for a few minutes more. Remove the ingredients from the pan and rest them on kitchen paper. Keeping the heat low, add the flour and mix it into the juices. Slowly add the red wine and stock.

Return the chicken and other cooked ingredients to the pan, add the bay leaves and bring to the boil. Cover and simmer gently for about 40 minutes.

To finish, carefully pour the red wine sauce into a smaller pan and bring to the boil again. Reduce the liquid by half. Reunite with the chicken and vegetables on a serving plate. Sprinkle with chopped parsley and tuck in. Bon appetit.

AUTUMN EN CROUTE
WITH CREAMED SPINACH

This is a lovely dish to bring to the table. It's colourful and majestic, yet really simple. Make no excuses for using shop-bought pastry, particularly if you have gone to the trouble of foraging your own mushrooms. The red peppers are better skinned: peppers can be a bit tough otherwise. I do this by blistering the skins in a gas flame, then rinsing them under the tap.

When you serve the pie at the table the red and orange of the peppers and squash will complement the vibrant green of the spinach. The squash will have shape yet softness and the melted cheese brings a delightful saltiness. The walnuts add crunch and the pastry soaks up the creamy spinach juices. Even the most committed carnivore won't miss the meat in this dish, particularly as the mushrooms are so succulent.

SERVES 4

for the pastry parcel
400g puff pastry
neck end 1 butternut squash, peeled and halved lengthways
2 red peppers, skinned and sliced
2 field mushrooms, thickly sliced
150g soft goat's cheese
70g walnuts, chopped
1 egg, beaten, for glazing

for the spinach
200g spinach, washed
100g unsalted butter
100ml double cream
nutmeg, grated
salt and white pepper

Preheat the oven to 200°C/180°C fan/400°F/Gas mark 6. Roll out the pastry to approximately 40 × 30cm. Lay the squash slices end to end in the middle of the pastry, then lay the pepper slices on top of the squash. Follow with thick slices of mushroom. Crumble the goat's cheese over the top and scatter chopped walnuts in the gaps. Fold over the pastry to make a sealed parcel. Make a few holes in the top with a sharp knife and glaze the pastry with beaten egg. Carefully transfer the parcel onto a baking tray and cook in the oven for about 50 minutes. If the pastry starts to burn, reduce the heat a little.

Put the spinach in a saucepan with half the butter and a generous sprinkling of salt. Cover and cook over a medium heat for a few minutes. There will be enough residual water on the spinach leaves to help it wilt. When the spinach has softened, pour off any excess liquid and add the cream, keeping the saucepan on a low heat to warm it through. Before serving add the rest of the butter, a grind of white pepper and a generous grating of nutmeg.

Onions

....

The humble onion gets a raw deal. In times gone by it has been worshipped, considered an aphrodisiac and even used as currency. Oh, how the mighty have fallen. Today we just take it for granted. We use it in curries and pies, chillies and pasta dishes, but seldom is it the star event. These recipes celebrate the dependable allium.

Onions do seem to hang around forever. They are one of the first crops to be planted and if you have a good year they are still lurking about after Christmas. Most veg are infinitely better if you eat them straight away. Onions (and other alliums) are more of an investment in the future. Left to dry – first on the soil from which they've been harvested, and later hung up in a garage or shed – their flavour mellows and matures. This is just as well: imagine the tears you would shed if you had to eat them all just after harvest. Young onions are infinitely more juicy and will make you cry more. A white salad onion is perfect in the summer, but it's reassuring to know that as the outer layers crisp and dry, they seal in fantastic flavour.

We may no longer worship onions, but I can't help but be grateful for the fact that we can so easily grow them – and in culinary terms I just don't know where we would be without them.

RED ONION JAM

I've always struggled with the name 'red onion marmalade', simply because it's red rather than orange, and so, in my desire for an uncomplicated view of the world, I feel it should be called jam.

Slicing so many onions can be a tear-jerking business. Red onions have a particularly strong effect on me and if I peeled and sliced the quantity this recipe requires my eyes would be redder than the onions. So I bow to technology: in a few minutes the food processor will slice them all, without so much as a whimper. Do cut out the hard root first though. You will need a 500ml storage jar (Kilner or an equivalent) which must be sterile and have an airtight lid. I keep this in the refrigerator, where it lasts for a couple of months.

MAKES 1 500ml JAR

50ml olive oil
700g red onions, thinly sliced
3 cloves garlic,
   roughly chopped
1 bouquet garni
   (rosemary and bay leaves)

4 cloves
2 teaspoons chilli powder
100g light brown sugar
100ml sherry vinegar
100ml red wine
salt

Heat the oil in a large saucepan over a low heat. Add the onions with a very generous sprinkling of salt. Stir for about ten minutes, so all the onions have a chance to soften. Add the garlic, bouquet garni and the cloves. After another ten minutes, the onions will start to go gloopy and break down. Add the chilli powder and sugar and stir into the mix until they are dissolved, then add the sherry vinegar and wine.

Allow the mixture to bubble away gently for about 15 minutes until most of the liquid has been absorbed by the onions and the syrup is thick and viscous. Remove from the heat, take out the cloves and the bouquet garni and allow to cool. Transfer the jam to the storage jar and seal.

WHITE ONION MARMALADE

I love it when a plan comes together. This started as an experiment, but I will make it regularly from now on. It's particularly useful to use up large white salad onions, which don't keep as well as ordinary white onions. I have tried making this dish with both and the salad onions give it a more delicate texture.

This marmalade has such an intense citrus note that I'm almost tempted to spread it on toast for breakfast, as well as lavishing it on white crumbly cheese for a late night snack.

MAKES 1 300ml JAR

300g white onions, thinly sliced
8 cloves garlic, chopped
20ml olive oil
30g caster sugar
1 tablespoon clear honey

75ml white wine vinegar
1 tablespoon orange juice
zest ½ unwaxed lemon
zest ½ orange
salt

Heat a saucepan and soften the onions and garlic in the oil over a low heat with a good sprinkling of salt. Cook for about ten minutes, until they become translucent and soft. Add the sugar and let it dissolve before adding the honey, vinegar, orange juice and zest. Reduce slowly for 10–15 minutes over a low heat, until most of the liquid has been absorbed by the onions. Allow to cool and transfer to a sterile jar.

Variation: if you prefer a more subtle flavour, leave out the orange.

PICCALILLI WITH HAM ON THE SIDE

This probably shouldn't be called piccalilli at all, as it's not traditional. My recollections of piccalilli involve large florets of uncooked cauliflower in a radioactive-looking sauce. So let's call this a piccalilli-inspired recipe. To be fair, it does involve a luminous yellow sauce, it is pickle and it does end up in a jar. Rather than use cauliflower, which I tend to harvest later in the season, I find this a fantastic recipe for using up any members of the onion family that look as though they won't make it through to winter, some windfall apples and the last of the courgettes or marrows. A ham hock helps the piccalilli disappear fast.

I have not kept a jar of this piccalilli long enough to know how long it keeps. Unopened, I'd say it should keep for a fairly long time. It's effectively vinegar and strong spices – I think our ancestors got away with such preservatives for years! In my house it disappears in days.

Small is beautiful for me in this recipe and the secret is to chop each ingredient into chunks small enough to allow a piece of each in every mouthful.

600g courgettes or marrow,
   cubed

300g red onions, cubed

100g mild white onions, cubed

200g shallots, cubed

6 large cloves garlic, cubed

3cm piece root ginger,
   peeled and cut into slivers

100g sugar

600ml white wine vinegar

6 cloves

3 medium apples,
   skins on, cubed

1 tablespoon plain flour

300ml water

8 teaspoons turmeric

1 tablespoon Dijon mustard

2 teaspoons cinnamon

salt

for the ham hock

1 ham hock (approx. 1kg) soaked overnight in cold water

1 medium onion, chopped

2 sticks celery, chopped

1 carrot, chopped

2 bay leaves

crusty roll, to serve

Sprinkle the courgettes, onions, shallots and garlic with salt and leave to one side for about ten minutes. Rinse them, and then put the onions, shallots and garlic into a large saucepan with the ginger and sugar and pour in the white wine vinegar. Cover the saucepan and bring the liquid to a simmer for five minutes, then add the cloves.

Add the courgettes to the saucepan. Simmer for five more minutes before adding the apple for a further 3–4 minutes. The point of the simmering is to cook the ingredients until tender, but not so long that they go mushy, so check and adjust the cooking time accordingly. Remove the pan from the heat and fish out the cloves. Drain the mixture and put the vinegar to one side.

Make a paste with the flour and a little water, put into a large saucepan and cook over a low heat. Gradually pour in the remaining water and the reserved vinegar and use a hand whisk to ensure the liquid is lump free. Add the turmeric, mustard and cinnamon and keep whisking: aim for a slightly thick liquid, the consistency of double cream. Turn off the heat and add the pickled vegetables, ensuring that each is coated in the sauce. Carefully fill the sterilised jars, pushing down the mixture and tapping each jar to get rid of air bubbles. Seal the jars and keep them in the refrigerator.

For the ham hock, drain the soaked hock and put it into the largest saucepan you have, then cover with water. Add the onion, celery and carrot to the pan with the bay leaves. Gently bring to the boil and simmer slowly for three hours. If any salt or impurities bubble to the surface, skim them off.

Turn off the heat and leave the ham to rest in the stock for 20 minutes. Remove the hock and allow it to cool before pulling off hunks to enjoy with a crusty roll and plenty of piccalilli.

ONION SOUP
WITH SHALLOT AND CHEESE CROUTONS

*I first made onion soup to use up a mountainous harvest. Ever since,
I have looked forward to the soft, velvety texture and intense sweet
flavour that this wonderful, understated vegetable can produce.
As before, you may prefer to use a food processor to chop the onions.*

SERVES 4–6

250g unsalted butter
30ml olive oil
2kg onions, chopped
8 cloves garlic, chopped
bunch thyme, tied with string
2 bay leaves
30ml balsamic vinegar
2 litres beef stock

4 medium shallots,
    finely chopped
1 French stick, cut diagonally
    into 2cm thick slices
100g Gruyère, grated,
    plus extra for serving
salt and freshly ground
    black pepper

Melt most of the butter and oil in a large saucepan over a
gentle heat. Put the onions and garlic in the pan and sprinkle
them with salt. Add the thyme and bay leaves. Cover the
pan and let the onions sweat for ten minutes until they are
translucent and soft.

Add the balsamic vinegar and stir, then slowly pour in the
stock. Simmer for 20 minutes. Melt the rest of the butter in a
frying pan and sauté the shallots until soft, then remove them
from the pan. Add the rest of the oil, then fry the French stick
slices so they are coloured on both sides (hot oil is essential to
avoid soggy bread). Spread the shallots on each crouton and
top with some grated Gruyère. Toast under a hot grill until
the cheese melts.

To serve, ladle a mixture of onions and juice into bowls and
top each with a crouton. Sprinkle some extra Gruyère on top
and add a grind of pepper.

Potatoes (maincrop)

By autumn, all the growing is done and the soil is just a protective blanket for the fully developed tubers. It's always a bit of a dilemma as to whether or not to harvest all the remaining spuds. If left in the claggy soil, they are much more likely to attract slugs, or if it's really wet, they may rot, but there is something nice about just digging them when you need them. Inevitably, even if I attempt to dig all the spuds in one go and dry them in an organised fashion, I miss loads and continue to find more for months. I'm convinced that potatoes taste fresher when preserved in the soil and anyway, a barrowful of newly dug spuds on Christmas Eve is fast turning into a tradition in my house. Once the digging up of organised rows is over, harvesting becomes more of a lottery, so I may set out with the intention of finding potatoes to roast, but uncover a few beauties that are perfect for baking. Then there are the half-eaten ones and the mis-shapes – they usually need a careful bit of sculpting with the knife or have 'mash me' written all over them.

RIB-EYE STEAK WITH THICK CHIPS

If you are going to the expense of buying steak, it's worth taking the time to make it a special dish all round. My mum used to cook chips like this; it takes a while but the results are worth it. Let's face it, it has taken months to grow the potatoes in the first place, so a few extra minutes of cooking is not too much to ask, is it?

SERVES 4

1.5kg floury potatoes, peeled and cut into long, thumb-width chips
4 cloves garlic, unpeeled
30ml rapeseed oil
8 shallots, finely chopped
1 red onion, thinly sliced
20ml olive oil
4 thick rib-eye steaks
50g unsalted butter
20ml red wine vinegar
salt and freshly ground white pepper

Put the chips in a large saucepan, cover with cold water and salt generously. Pop in the garlic cloves. Bring to the boil and simmer for about eight minutes, until the potatoes have softened but not become mushy. Drain, put the garlic to one side and put a lid on the pan so the potatoes continue to steam for a few minutes. Carefully transfer them onto a clean tea towel to dry out completely.

Take a large frying pan and add enough rapeseed oil to come halfway up the side. Heat over a medium heat and cook the chips in batches for about five minutes – they should cook through and take on a light crust. Carefully put them to one side on kitchen paper until the steak is ready.

Put the shallots and onion with the olive oil and a pinch of salt in the largest frying pan you have, over a medium heat. Sweat them until they are soft, then remove from the pan and put to one side.

Season the steaks on both sides, with salt and white pepper. Melt the butter in the residue of oil still in the frying pan and turn up the heat until the butter bubbles. Add the steaks and cook for roughly 3–4 minutes on each side. Put the steaks to one side, but keep them warm. Return the onion and shallots to the pan and squeeze in the paste from the garlic cloves. Turn up the heat and use the red wine vinegar to mix all the flavours in the pan. Reduce so that the liquid becomes thick and sticky, while you finish the chips.

Reheat the chip oil until it is spitting hot. Carefully add the chips in batches and cook for about five minutes until they are crisp and golden.

To serve, put a steak on one side of each plate and spoon over some of the viscous jus with the soft onion and shallots. Pile the other side of each plate high with chips and sprinkle them with salt.

ALMOST PERFECT ROASTIES

Some chefs will tell you that perfect roast potatoes need goose fat. They may well be right, but it's not something I usually have in the cupboard. For me, perfect roasties require freshly dug potatoes. Those I do have. I can get them from earth to plate in under an hour and even though I admit I have never compared freshly dug potatoes with those that have been lying around for a few weeks, I'm convinced that they have a unique flavour. Desiree or King Edward are my usual choice for their fluffy soft interiors and I use a pressure cooker for the initial cooking.

SERVES 6

1.5kg potatoes, peeled and halved lengthways
300ml vegetable oil
salt

Preheat the oven to 220°C/200°C/425°F/Gas mark 7. Put the potatoes into a pressure cooker of salted water, turn on the heat and cook for ten minutes. If you are using an ordinary saucepan, give them 15 minutes. As always, much depends on the size of the spud: don't overcook them. The aim is to partially cook the potatoes and soften the outsides. Meanwhile, pour the oil into a roasting tin and put it in the oven.

Drain the potatoes and allow them to steam dry for a few moments. Give the pan a vigorous shake with the lid on to soften the outside of the potatoes further before carefully tipping them into the roasting tin of sizzling oil. Gently shake the tray to ensure that each potato is coated in oil and then sprinkle with salt. Put the roasting tin back into the oven for 40 minutes. Halfway through check the potatoes and turn them over. They should be crisp on the outside and fluffy and light inside.

SAUSAGES AND MASH
WITH THICK RED ONION GRAVY

If you get this dish right, nothing can beat it. For perfect mash use floury potatoes such as Desiree, Maris Piper or King Edward. Ideally, the sausages should be slightly sticky, the mash creamy and mustardy and the onions soft, velvety, sweet and mushy. Where the onions end and the gravy begins is hard to pinpoint, but the slightly acidic runny jus will be soaked up by the mash and mingle with the molten butter.

SERVES 4

1.5kg potatoes, peeled and cut into chunks
2 large onions, chopped
2 cloves garlic, chopped
10ml vegetable oil
200g unsalted butter
1 bay leaf
30ml balsamic vinegar
750ml vegetable stock
12 good quality sausages
30ml milk
1 tablespoon Dijon mustard
salt
steamed leeks, to serve

Boil the potatoes in a saucepan of salted water until a knife glides through them easily. Drain and cover them.

Heat a large frying pan and gently sauté the onions and garlic in the oil. Add a pinch of salt and when the onions start to become translucent melt about 30g of the butter in the pan. Add the bay leaf and continue to cook slowly for ten minutes until the onions are gloopy. Add the balsamic vinegar and the stock and turn up the heat a little, so it starts to bubble.

Grill the sausages under a medium heat, turning regularly. There's no need to prick them; the fat will find its own way out.

Mash the potatoes with 50g of butter, the milk and the mustard.

To serve, heap some mash in the middle of each plate. Adorn with yet more butter (more than you think is decent). Arrange three sausages symmetrically on the mash and ladle on some soft onions and gravy. Accompany with a generous pile of steamed leek.

'EEL TAPS 'N' EGGS

I grew up with this dish. 'Eel taps are thin slices of potato, fried until crisp and golden on the outside and soft inside. They are named after the shape of the heel on a shoe. It took me until I was a teenager to realise this, having previously thought that it had something to do with slippery fish and plumbing.

As each decade of my life has passed, 'eel taps have been a trusted and worthy companion. Whether eaten mid-morning as a late breakfast, or late at night after a few too many beers or now as a father with a hungry mouth to feed from an almost empty refrigerator, they always deliver.

SERVES 1

400g potatoes, peeled and thinly sliced
20ml vegetable oil
2 eggs
80g extra mature Cheddar, grated
salt and black pepper

Sprinkle the potato slices with salt, then heat a heavy-based frying pan and fry the slices in hot oil for a few minutes. Flip the slices as they start to colour to make sure that they are cooked on both sides. Lower the heat and make room in the pan for the eggs. Crack them in and when cooked, transfer the contents of the pan to a plate, with the Cheddar and some black pepper.

Variation: this works equally well with partially boiled potatoes; just cook them for less time and slice them a little thicker. If you have some in the refrigerator, add some slices of chorizo sausage.

TAPAS (aka TATTY TAPAS)

There are some spuds that are so far from being perfect (misshapen, inhabited or pierced by the fork) that it would be easy to just discard them. To do so is a crime against creativity and a missed opportunity. When I see the leftovers from a crop of harvested spuds, I imagine a feast – a fabulous meal in which these potatoes star as the perfect dish. They may be small and irregular, but they become the starting point for delicious tapas – a fine feast which transforms every last scrap in the refrigerator and veg box into an elaborate and delicious plate. These small plates can share the same oven and table.

Patatas bravas

SERVES 2

500g potatoes, peeled
    and cut into 2cm cubes
20ml olive oil
2 large ripe tomatoes,
    finely chopped
1 teaspoon sugar

2 cloves garlic, quartered
sprig thyme
20ml lemon juice
salt and freshly ground
    black pepper

Preheat the oven to 200°C/180°C fan/400°F/Gas mark 6. Drizzle the potato cubes with olive oil and sprinkle with salt. Put them in a roasting tin and cook in the hot oven for 20 minutes.

Sprinkle the tomatoes with the sugar, and add them and their juice to the roasting tin, making sure that each potato cube is coated. Nestle the garlic chunks evenly among the potatoes. Pop the sprig of thyme into the dish and sprinkle the lemon juice over it.

Put the roasting tin back in the oven for a further 20 minutes. The potatoes will crisp and the tomato will start to bubble and caramelise on the edges of the dish. Serve with a grind of black pepper.

Heavenly sticky sausages

SERVES 2

2 tablespoons clear honey
1 tablespoon Dijon mustard
8 chipolatas
8 rashers streaky bacon

Mix the honey and mustard and smother each sausage with the mixture before rolling it in a streaky bacon blanket. Bake in the oven alongside the potatoes for around 20 minutes.

Lamb nuggets

SERVES 2

15g dried apricots, finely chopped
15g almond flakes, lightly crushed
4 anchovies, chopped

1 tablespoon chopped mint
250g minced lamb
juice and zest 1 lime
2 tablespoons clear honey
150g Greek yoghurt, to serve

In a large bowl mix the apricots, almond flakes, anchovies, mint and lamb mince. Get stuck in with your hands and mix them all together. Add the lime juice and shape the mixture into bite-sized meatballs. Glaze the outside of each meatball with a little honey and put them in the oven (alongside the potatoes and sausages) for 20 minutes. Finely chop the lime zest and mix into the Greek yoghurt. Drizzle a little honey over the yoghurt to make a dip for the meatballs when cooked.

Rosemary

....

I have a fantastic rosemary bush on the allotment. It's been with me for years, first in a progression of pots of varying sizes, then in a very fertile patch in the corner of the plot. This may be related to the fact that this was where manure deliveries were once made. Anyhow, there it has flourished and so I am never short of huge handfuls of very woody, extremely oily aromatic stems and leaves. The plant is so robust, yet I know that a severe winter frost could end my relationship with it overnight. Around this time of year, when the frosts threaten, I always have a little panic and overdose on rosemary-related recipes.

HAKE WITH CAPERS
IN A LEMON AND ROSEMARY SAUCE

Rosemary is not an obvious partner for fish, but it absolutely works. If you use plenty, the aromatic oils infuse the fish. The subtle flavour of the rosemary complements the fresh lemon and the salty capers and brings a little Mediterranean magic to the windiest of autumnal evenings.

SERVES 2

4 sprigs rosemary,
  plus a few leaves to serve
4 cloves garlic
1 lemon, thickly sliced
2 hake fillets
  (approx. 150g each)

20ml lemon juice
100g unsalted butter
4 shallots, chopped
20g capers
zest ½ unwaxed lemon,
  to serve

Take two pieces of aluminium foil at least twice the size of the fish fillets and make a foil parcel for each fillet. On each piece of foil put a couple of sprigs of rosemary, two cloves of garlic and a thick slice of lemon. Lay the fish on top, drizzle with half the lemon juice and seal the parcels. Put them in the top of a steamer and steam for around 15 minutes.

In a frying pan, sauté the shallots in half the butter until soft. Add the capers and the remaining lemon juice and bring to a simmer. Just before serving, add a few finely chopped rosemary leaves and the rest of the butter. Allow to warm through for a few minutes, then serve with the steamed fish topped with lemon zest.

ROSEMARY ROAST POTATOES WITH GARLIC, CHORIZO AND MOZZARELLA

When I do a random dig and uncover a hotchpotch of potato varieties, I often resort to this quick, easy and thoroughly delicious brunch. Having potatoes with different textures and flavours is a bonus. This is a bold dish, rustic in appearance and I suggest bringing the roasting tin to the table when serving it. The creamy cheese, hot potatoes and spicy sausage are a fantastic combination. It's not what I'd call a balanced meal, but it is likely to provoke requests for second helpings. Once you've eaten the first mouthful you won't be able to stop until the dish is empty. The potatoes will, to varying degrees, have absorbed the paprika-flavoured juices from the chorizo. Some will be soft and squidgy; others a little firmer. The cheese will stretch and melt in the residual heat.

SERVES 2

750g potatoes, peeled, unpeeled or both, depending on your preference, sliced into golf ball-sized chunks

olive oil, for drizzling

150g chorizo, cut into 1cm chunks

4 cloves garlic, halved

20ml lemon juice

a few sprigs rosemary

1 ball mozzarella, torn into bite-sized chunks

salt and freshly ground black pepper

Preheat the oven to 200°C/180°C fan/400°F/Gas mark 6. Put the potato slices in a roasting tin, drizzle with olive oil, sprinkle with salt and put in the oven. After 15 minutes, give the tin a good shake to make sure that none of the spuds have stuck to the bottom. Add the chorizo and garlic, distributing them evenly through the tin. Sprinkle over half the lemon juice and snuggle a few sprigs of rosemary among the potatoes. Roast for a further 40 minutes.

Remove the rosemary and arrange the mozzarella pieces evenly through the tin. Grind black pepper over everything and give a final sprinkling of lemon juice and olive oil before serving.

Squash and pumpkins

Squash and pumpkins are such a joy. Tired autumn leaves may swirl around the plot, but the pumpkin patch clings onto summer. For much of the year these large balls of colour have been quietly swelling, while all the attention has been on the other crops. Then, when the summer sunshine starts to fade, the oranges, creams, reds and yellows of the pumpkins and squashes begin to deepen and glow against the earth. I love the fact that both are sprawling plants. No matter where they start out on the plot, their long eager shoots invade and entwine. As they grow, the odd fruit randomly matures here and there. The resulting jungle of plants leaves a network of varied shapes, sizes and colours dotted over a large area. Only when the leaves start to die back does a clear picture of the size and quality of the crop emerge.

Picking a heavy ball of deliciousness and tramping to the wheelbarrow with it feels like such a personal achievement. I feel like a proud child when harvesting squash. Pushing a wheelbarrow full of sunshine past allotment neighbours on

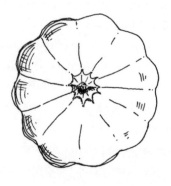

a windy autumn day is like collecting a medal on sports day. I was never fast enough for that, but I've got over it.

I could fill a book with squash and pumpkin recipes alone, not least because I grow several varieties and each has its own quirks. Butternut squashes and jack-o'-lantern pumpkins always do well, but I also love the texture of a spaghetti squash, the meatiness of a Marina di Chioggia or Futsu; the creaminess of a Tan Cheese or Cream of the Crop and the nutmeg hints of a Moschata.

One of my favourite things about pumpkins and squashes is that every last bit can be used. Many of my recipes include the skins, and the seeds are delicious toasted or dried. A few years ago I would have discarded them, but I noticed a bag appeared in our shopping trolley the other day, so now the seeds are used too.

BUTTERNUT SQUASH SOUP

This recipe is so easy that making it can hardly be classed as cooking. It's not the simplicity that attracts me though, it's the fact that I use every bit of the fruit, with nothing ending up on the compost heap. I often harvest four or five squashes from one plant: it's amazing to think that the fruit from one small seed could feed more than 20 people.

SERVES 4

1 butternut squash or small pumpkin, chopped into golf ball-sized chunks, seeds reserved

2 red chillies

4 cloves garlic

oil, for drizzling

1 litre chicken stock

splash balsamic vinegar

salt and pepper

chilli sauce (optional)

Preheat the oven to 200°C/180°C fan/400°F/Gas mark 6. Put the squash in a roasting tin with the whole chillies and garlic cloves. Drizzle with oil and rub to ensure that each piece is coated. Sprinkle with salt and pepper. Bake in the oven for 40 minutes.

When the pieces are soft, blitz them in a blender, gradually adding the hot stock. You may need to do this in batches. Pour into a large saucepan and warm through on a low heat.

Rinse the seeds in a colander, then sprinkle with salt and the balsamic vinegar. Pop under the grill for ten minutes to toast. Shake them halfway through the cooking time so that both sides turn a golden hue. Use them to top the soup, perhaps with the tiniest drizzle of olive oil, or chilli sauce if you prefer. Eat the rest of the seeds as nibbles.

FRIGHTENINGLY GOOD PUMPKIN STEW

Pumpkin stew is an appropriate treat for a spooky Halloween night. It's a lot thicker and heartier than the squash soups I make and is really filling. I must admit I'm boringly strict about not using my organically grown fruits for making scary pumpkin heads. I'm more than happy to go to the supermarket for those, but I'm delighted to make a big pan of home-grown pumpkin stew to mark the occasion. Inevitably, there is a lot of pumpkin stew eaten in our house, due to the frequently abundant harvest of pumpkins and squashes.

Pumpkin isn't the easiest fruit in the world to peel; I usually find that cutting it into sections first helps. Then it's easier to scoop out the flesh, as you would with a melon.

SERVES 4

20ml olive oil
2 medium red onions, chopped
2 large carrots, cubed
1 stick celery, cubed
**1 medium pumpkin, peeled,
    cut into large chunks**

1 litre vegetable stock
200g red lentils
150ml cream
crusty bread, to serve

Heat the oil in a heavy saucepan over a medium heat. Gently sweat the onions in it until soft. Add the carrots, celery and pumpkin and cook for a few minutes before adding the stock and lentils. Cover and simmer for about half an hour, until the lentils are cooked through. Use a slotted spoon to remove the pumpkin chunks, then put everything else in a food processor and blitz until smooth. Return the liquid to the saucepan and replace the pumpkin pieces. Stir in the cream and serve hot with crusty bread.

WARM GOAT'S CHEESE, SQUASH AND RED ONION SALAD

Eating a salad in the autumn feels like a defiant act. It's a denial that summer is over; a stubborn gesture to keep the sun shining. This salad lights up the plate and is hearty enough to nourish the soul on a rainy evening. The combination of the warm, salty goat's cheese and the sweet, soft squash is reflected in the dressing, with sweet honey and sour lemon juice pulling the flavours together. Walnuts and baby gem add a welcome crunch to the softer ingredients.

SERVES 4

1 small squash, cut into bite-sized pieces
30ml vegetable oil
2 medium red onions, quartered
4 cloves garlic, whole
2 sprigs thyme

1 tablespoon clear honey
juice 1 lemon
50ml extra-virgin olive oil
200g soft goat's cheese, sliced
1 baby gem lettuce
50g walnut halves

Preheat the oven to 200°C/180°C fan/400°F/Gas mark 6. Put the squash pieces in a roasting tin and coat them in the vegetable oil, then roast for 40 minutes. At the halfway stage, pop in the red onions, garlic and thyme.

Next make the dressing. Put the honey, lemon and olive oil into a screw-topped jam jar, put on the lid and shake the jar vigorously. Toast the goat's cheese for five minutes under a hot grill until it starts to blister. Assemble the salad with the lettuce leaves at the bottom and the toasted cheese, warm squash, onion, garlic and walnuts on top. Finally drizzle on the dressing.

BUTTERNUT SQUASH, FENNEL AND RED PEPPER WITH COUSCOUS

Make a lot of this dish: it makes a perfect effortless evening meal and a delicious lunch the next day. The sweetness of the squash and peppers complement each other and the fennel adds a lovely aroma and warmth to the dish.

I tend to save up pumpkin and squash seeds and cook them in batches, either roasted or grilled. They keep well in airtight containers and are a great snack in their own right, but also add texture and nuttiness to all sorts of soups and salads.

SERVES 4

½ butternut squash, cut into finger-length chunks, seeds reserved

30ml olive oil, plus extra for drizzling and frying

splash soy sauce

2 large fennel bulbs, cut into finger-length chunks

4 red peppers, quartered

4 cloves garlic, peeled and left whole

30ml lemon juice

1 stick celery, finely chopped

400ml vegetable stock

300g couscous (ideally large grain)

salt

Preheat the oven to 170°C/150°C fan/325°F/Gas mark 3. Wash and dry the squash seeds. Drizzle oil over them, plus some salt and a splash of soy sauce, then spread them over a baking tray. Pop into the oven for about 30 minutes until roasted.

Increase the oven temperature to 200°C/180°C fan/400°F/ Gas mark 6. Put the squash, fennel and peppers on a roasting tray with the garlic cloves. Drizzle with the lemon juice and oil and give the tray a shake so that everything is evenly coated. Roast in the oven for about 30 minutes.

Heat a large saucepan and soften the celery in a little hot oil, then add the stock. Bring to the boil. Put the couscous in a bowl and pour the liquid over it, then cover and leave it for 15 minutes. When the couscous has absorbed the stock, remove the cover and drizzle olive oil over it, stirring it with a fork to separate the grains. Carefully mix the couscous and roasted vegetables, so the veg still keeps its shape. Arrange on a serving plate and finish with the squash seeds.

BAKED CUSTARD WHITE SQUASH WITH LEEKS, GARLIC AND PARMESAN

Forgive me if you haven't come across this variety of squash; it may not be readily available in food shops. However, it is well worthwhile hunting down; if you can get your hands on a custard white squash, cook it – it's a wonderful ingredient with a taste like no other. This squash makes a light alternative to potato or just an interesting side vegetable. If you manage to get your hands on more than one, try alternative fillings. It soaks up the flavour of anything you put inside it – chilli and herbs also work well. To prepare a custard white squash, cut a circle approximately ten centimetres in diameter around the stem and remove a plug. Keep the plug to one side and scoop out the seeds.

SERVES 4 AS A SIDE DISH

1 custard white squash,
  seeds removed and
  plug reserved
20g unsalted butter

1 medium leek,
  very finely chopped
3 cloves garlic, finely chopped
50g Parmesan, grated

Preheat the oven to 200°C/180°C fan/400°F/Gas mark 6. Put half the butter into the squash cavity, followed by the leeks, garlic and Parmesan. Top with the remaining butter and replace the plug in the hole. Put the squash on a baking tray and bake in the oven for 30–40 minutes. Serve at the table by scooping out the leeks with a mound of the soft, sweet white flesh, infused with the butter, Parmesan and garlic.

SPAGHETTI SQUASH ITALIANO

I always seem to do well with spaghetti squash. If you don't, they can often be picked up at farmers' markets and are a welcome addition to the autumn table. As the name suggests, the squash flesh resembles spaghetti when cooked. Long clear strings absorb flavours and make a statement on the plate. It looks like a plate of pasta, but it's much lighter in texture and I would guess contains fewer calories too. To prepare the squash, cut off the top third with a sharp knife, as if taking the top off a boiled egg. Scoop out the seeds to use later and keep the top to use as a lid. Cut a thin slice off the base to help it stand up.

SERVES 4 AS A SIDE OR STARTER

20g unsalted butter
12 cherry tomatoes
1 medium onion, finely chopped
4 cloves garlic, finely chopped
bunch basil, chopped

1 spaghetti squash, top and seeds removed, top reserved
10ml lemon juice
grated Parmesan, to serve
salt and freshly ground black pepper

Preheat the oven to 200°C/180°C fan/400°F/Gas mark 6. Put the butter, tomatoes, onion, garlic and basil into the squash with a splash of lemon juice and replace the lid. Place the squash upright on a baking tray and bake in the oven for 40–50 minutes. Serve at the table: as with pasta, you will need to push a fork into the strands and twist it. To complete the Italian illusion, accompany with a good sprinkling of Parmesan and some freshly ground black pepper.

LAMB NECK FILLETS
WITH SQUASH AND POTATOES

This is one of the cheaper cuts of lamb, but full of flavour. It can be really tender if cooked slowly. The squash and potatoes literally melt in the pot and absorb the succulent lamb juices. It's one of the dishes I look forward to from the moment I plant the squash seeds.

SERVES 4–6

lamb neck fillets,
 about 200–250g each

8 anchovies

20ml olive oil

plain flour, for dusting

20g thyme leaves, chopped

600g small waxy potatoes,
 sliced in 2cm thick slices

½ butternut squash, seeded
 but not peeled

1 bay leaf

3 cloves garlic, left whole

375ml red wine

200ml water

salt and pepper

Preheat the oven to 170°C/150°C fan/325°F/Gas mark 3. Make small incisions in the fillets and poke the anchovies into them. Rub the fillets in oil, season with salt and pepper and coat in flour and thyme leaves. Heat a heavy-based frying pan and seal the fillets on all sides for a few minutes, until the lamb takes on a deep colour.

Put the potato and squash pieces into an ovenproof dish along with the bay leaf and garlic. Nestle the lamb fillets on top. Pour a large glass of red wine (around 250ml) into the frying pan and mix together all the juices. Pour them into the dish along with another glass of red wine (around 125ml) and the water. Put on the lid and bake in the oven for 1½–2 hours. Let the lamb fillets rest for ten minutes before serving. The potatoes and squash will be soft and the lamb tender – a perfect autumn dish.

It gets even darker
before it gets lighter...

It was fortuitous that Guy Fawkes tried to blow up parliament when he did because 5 November is the perfect milestone for clearing the debris of the season and preparing the ground for the next growing year. If it wasn't completely the wrong time of year, this could be described as a spring clean. I guess it's more akin to 'the morning after the night before'. You can look back at the party and remember the good bits, but you don't want the empty bottles hanging around any longer.

In preparation for a Bonfire Night frenzy, I attempt to get as much harvesting done as possible. That usually results in several weekends struggling with full wheelbarrows. By the end of the season, the pumpkin plants that were once mighty sprawlers will have withered. Any leftover pumpkins will be taken to a cool garage or shed, where they should last till Christmas.

Whilst I may not have much enthusiasm for planting, as the months progress the opportunity to put in broad beans and garlic comes ever closer and so does the prospect of a new year. It really pays to be thorough. The temptation in the cold months is to do a half-hearted dig over and get the garlic and beans in as quickly as possible. Do that and you will spend hours battling with weeds in the spring, and if you fail at that task, the plants will struggle to reach their best. It's much better to take a little longer now, pulling out roots or slivers of unwelcome guests and rogue plants. This is cold, lonely work, though. None of the friends who were so eager to pick strawberries and beans in the summer are as keen to visit now. I usually find a bowl of squash soup or pumpkin stew is an appropriate reward for my labours.

As autumn calms, the soil almost begs to be turned. As each heavy clod is turned over, the promise of the new season mentally germinates. Now when the wind screeches, it is drying the sods; the erratic swirling leaves no longer annoy but create a protective mulch. The darkness and intensity of the soil is a sign of richness and fertility, rather than a barren space. Where others may see desolation the gardener sees hope and potential. It's not a bad outlook on life.

The winter vegetables keep growing, of course. The next few months help to mature and intensify the flavours of these tough guys of the neighbourhood. Parsnips in particular relish a bit of cold and the greens shrug off the frosts effortlessly.

Now the heat has gone completely from the day and winter draws ever closer, the remaining potatoes, onions and – dare I admit – cabbages will be comforting winter companions. Along with the roots, they will loyally bridge the gap of the hungry months until the seed catalogues land on the door mat and the first salad sowings herald the start of a whole new season and whatever that may bring.

Winter

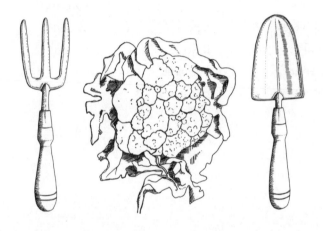

What to plant and harvest in winter

Plant

broad beans   garlic

Harvest

beetroot	hardy greens	sprouts
cabbages	kale	swedes
cauliflowers	leeks	turnips
celeriac	parsnips	
chard	potatoes	

WINTER RECIPES

Beetroot

Balsamic roasted beetroot
with Wensleydale, sour cream and chives
Blood-red risotto

Cabbage

Savoy cabbage
Savoy cabbage with leeks, bacon and eggs
Two-tone cabbage stir-fry with prawns and ginger
Breast of lamb with onions and red cabbage
Pickled cabbage, walnut and goat's cheese salad

Cauliflower

Curry with chickpeas and cauliflower
Cauliflower cheese

Celeriac

Baked honey salmon fillet with celeriac purée
Celeriac chips with venison cutlets

Leeks

Leek tops with chicken, white wine and mustard

Creamed leeks with Parmesan on toast

Leek, mushroom and bacon risotto

Prawn and leek spaghetti

Pork fillet stuffed with dates and leeks

Mussels with cider and leeks

Leek and potato soup

Chicken, leek and mushroom pie
with spinach and carrots

Sprouts, kale and hardy greens

Sprouts, apples and bacon

Whiting with chorizo and spicy kale

Christmas burger with bubble and squeak patties

Swedes, turnips and parsnips

Haggis, creamed potato
and bashed neeps with whisky sauce

Turnips and lardons

Winter chicken casserole

Spicy parsnip rosti with chilli sauce

Honey and cumin parsnips

Winter roast chicken with roastie rooties

Indulging in discontent…

During the shortest days of winter, the allotment landscape is at its most harsh and arguably its most beautiful. The hardy greens stand defiant against the elements, but there are few other signs of life, apart from the persistent hungry robin. However, the sparseness has its own charm and majesty.

The Christmas lights might well be twinkling in the high street, while the supermarkets bulge with festive bargains and the television pours out gift ideas and seasonal jingles, but there is no experience quite so reassuring and sobering in the days leading up to Christmas as an afternoon on the allotment. It's cold, bleak, tinsel-free and magically still and quiet.

As the fork pierces the dark, crisp soil, it's easy to be mentally transported back to the summer and memories of the crops that succeeded and the ghosts of those that failed; the tricks that nature played and the mistakes you made. In a wind's breath, the mind wanders to the future: a New Year, different seeds, ambitions and excitement about the oncoming growing season. Then, as the clods of earth are slowly turned, the mind is jolted back to Christmas Present. Almost miraculously, from what looks like a culinary wilderness, amazing food appears. It starts with random spuds uncovered by the spadeful. There are also still a scattering of leeks about. I have a healthy crop of carrots, turnips, beetroot, parsnips, celeriac and swedes, waiting for their moment to be harvested. The onions and garlic dried in the autumn will last for months. Then there are the brassicas: broccoli in all guises (purple sprouting being the most in vogue), but also cabbages, cauliflowers, sprouts and kale. In truth, if I have planted wisely, there is more than enough winter produce to devour.

However optimistic the soul, I admit it takes a big heart to actually fall in love with winter veg. Childhood experiences are to blame. The memory of school dinner halls wafting with the scent of watery mashed swede prompts nightmares to make the most stable of us reach for the therapist's number. And if aroma-induced flashbacks aren't enough, the recollection of Boxing Day white bread sandwiches swimming in blood-red vinegar does little to redeem the murdered beetroot's image.

Maybe, then, it's a sign of maturity that in recent years I have grown to cherish winter produce. I think it started with respect: let's face it, these veg thrive when the rest of us shiver – they deserve admiration. I'd say my winter veg are now as dear to me as their summer cousins. I relish the opportunity to cook and eat them. Harvesting them in torrents of rain and howling winds, though, still does little to cheer me.

However miserable the climate, my solace is in the knowledge that things will soon improve. The winter solstice (21 December), aka the shortest day, changes everything. Like love. Forgotten by most in the pre-Christmas madness, the sun quietly slips over the line and the days begin to claw back time from the nights. The countdown to spring is thus officially under way. Of course, it doesn't ever feel like that outside: nature saves some of its cruellest weather for January and February, so it's best not to get overly excited about the summer just yet. Christmas, though, is a worthy distraction from the cold because the cook knows that this is the time when true indulgence is not only allowed but expected.

When the only relics of Christmas are the yellow toffees left in the tin and the new socks have been put away in a drawer, it's time to look ahead once more. There's a new year, a new diet (of course) and – after an overdose of Christmas TV – a renewed vigour which compels me to get outside and take on nature for another growing season. There's much to do and things happen incredibly quickly. With the shortest day over, the garlic and broad beans soon dare to point their shoots through the soil, tempted to flourish but wary of the imminent February frosts. The soil lies quietly in anticipation of its first dig of the new year.

Ordering seeds never fails to bring a sense of hope and anticipation. It's practically impossible to think about a packet of seeds without allowing yourself the indulgence of contemplating what you will cook with the harvest from it. The fire flickers, the winter rain blasts the windows, yet I drift off into thoughts of long hot summer days of pea shoot salads, new potatoes with mint, runner beans in butter and a huge bowl of strawberries. It's going to be a good year. With seeds, it's always going to be a good year.

Beetroot

If there were ever a talent show for vegetables, beetroot would be the surprise act that everyone sniggers at as it takes the stage. Believe me, by the end of the performance, there would be a standing ovation. Sitting there in the mud, beetroots look dirty, tough and unkempt. After a quick wash, the peeler only has to nick the surface for the radiant and stunning colours to shine through. Spatter actually – all over the sink, worktops and usually my shirt. Despite the mess, it's impossible not to be impressed or excited by such colour. There are some fantastic varieties. My favourites are the deep red crimson Detroit types and the Italian Chioggia Barbabietola, which has amazing red and white rings when cut which are truly beautiful to look at.

Sadly, along with cabbage, I neglected beetroot for many years. I think it was that jar of pickled beetroot that came out every Boxing Day through my entire childhood. The stains on the Christmas tablecloth were an annual reminder of the thrills, spills and visitors of Christmasses past. I wonder what happened to that jar? I'm pretty sure nobody ever finished it.

Since growing a wide range of beetroots, I have new love for them. I appreciate their leaves in salad all summer long and I look forward to cooking the understated but ultimately magnificent globes in winter.

BALSAMIC ROASTED BEETROOT WITH WENSLEYDALE, SOUR CREAM AND CHIVES

A clutch of freshly harvested beetroot is an exciting prospect on a dark day. I often serve beetroot as a side to a hearty roast, but beetroots' beauty and flavour demand that they get the occasional leading role. Cooked long enough to be soft when bitten into, and sweetened by balsamic vinegar, the juices in this dish ooze into the crumbly cheese. It never fails to warm and cheer.

SERVES 4

500g beetroot, washed, skins on
20ml vegetable oil
20ml balsamic vinegar
25g chives, chopped

200ml sour cream
100g Wensleydale cheese
20g pine nuts, to serve
salt

Preheat the oven to 200°C/180°C fan/400°F/Gas mark 6. Put the beetroot in a saucepan of salted water and boil for 15 minutes. Rinse them in a bowl of cold water and peel off the skins. Cut them into golf ball-sized chunks and put them in an ovenproof dish. Add the oil, a little salt and the balsamic vinegar. With your hands, turn the pieces to ensure that each is well covered. Roast in the oven for 30–40 minutes, until a knife easily pierces them.

Put the chives in a mixing bowl with the sour cream. Stir together, then crumble in half the Wensleydale, ensuring that it is folded evenly through the mix.

Serve the beetroot on warm plates, with pieces of the remaining Wensleydale nestled amongst the crimson roots. Spoon over the cooking juices, sprinkle on a scattering of pine nuts and devour immediately.

BLOOD-RED RISOTTO

*This embarrassingly scarlet dish has all the creaminess of a risotto
but an after-kick of heat to die for. Try not to feel too guilty about
eating it – it's an innocent pleasure in my book.*

*I must warn you that after cooking this, the whole kitchen
may look like a crime scene. Your hands, the sink and walls will
portray carnage. As you scrub your hands, you will, to any passing
Shakespearean, resemble Lady Macbeth fretting to cleanse herself of
each dark spot. In my opinion it's well worth doing the time (cooking
and cleaning time, that is) for this. With its healthy ingredients, this
dish is likely to do you more good than harm – which is unusual for
an indulgence. The trouble is you may want more and more: once
you have tasted it, it'll be hard to shake off the attraction. A secret
beetroot habit might result.*

SERVES 2–3

20ml vegetable oil
100g unsalted butter
100g red cabbage, grated
2 cloves garlic, finely chopped
1 small red chilli, deseeded
   and finely chopped
1 large red onion,
   finely chopped

250g Arborio rice
175ml red wine
150g beetroot, grated
20ml balsamic vinegar
750ml chicken stock
2 teaspoons ground ginger
100g cream cheese

Heat the oil in a large saucepan and melt half the butter
into it. Add the red cabbage and stir for a few minutes before
adding the garlic, chilli, onion and rice. When all the rice is
coated and has been cooked for a few minutes, add the red
wine, beetroot and balsamic vinegar. Turn up the heat so
that the liquid bubbles, then reduce the heat again and
cover the saucepan.

   Heat the chicken stock in a separate saucepan. When the
liquid has nearly disappeared in the rice saucepan, sprinkle
in the ground ginger and add a ladleful of hot stock. Stir and
cover. When this liquid has been absorbed, add another

ladleful of stock. Stir and cover repeatedly until all the liquid has been absorbed and the rice is gloopy and soft. This will take about 20 minutes.

Just before serving, stir in the remaining butter and the cream cheese.

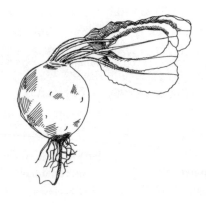

Cabbage

....

No matter how connected I might feel with my home-grown vegetables, I have to admit that sometimes winter cabbages look rough. Covered in holes, infested with slugs and looking lost and desolate, it's often tempting to just walk on by and leave the slugs to it. Thankfully I'm a bit too greedy for that. Anything that survives the pounding rain, wind, hail and sleet of winter should be given a second chance. The cabbages certainly need a good scrub and you need to keep watch for all inhabitants, but they are so worth the effort.

I have to 'fess up' that cabbage wasn't part of my life for many years, perhaps decades. We didn't fall out, we just drifted apart. More recently, I have managed to reconnect with it, despite its unpalatable reputation. Quite simply, the poor veg has a PR problem – the legacy of overcooked, mushy school dinners, which seriously cramps its style. Its unsavoury history triggers memories of a smelly school dining hall and un-identifiable matter left on the side of everyone's plates. Who can fail to remember how the pungent smell started to fill the school corridors from mid-morning and hung around all day? Overcooking cabbage is a sin: it completely destroys both flavour and texture, makes it nutritionally useless and gives generations nightmares. School dinners gave cabbage a bad name and I fear it has struggled ever since.

I only started growing it in order to have something other than weeds in the winter ground. Slowly and surely I have stopped judging it by my encounters with it in the past and after a short probationary period, I have now evangelically discovered the joy of cabbage.

SAVOY CABBAGE

This dish is the antithesis of mushy cabbage. I like to slightly undercook it. Savoy cabbage is a hardy soul, but beneath that tough exterior hides a wonderful distinctive flavour. I could eat a bowl of this on its own for dinner. This dish indulges the cabbage by bathing it in velvety butter, while allowing it to retain a little bite. The result is that the cabbage melts in the mouth rather than in the pan. Alongside a juicy pork chop, the cabbage will more than earn its place and the bowl will be emptied fast.

SERVES 4, AS A SIDE

1 Savoy cabbage, quartered, stalk removed, sliced into finger-width strips

30g unsalted butter, cut into small cubes

coarse sea salt and freshly ground white pepper

freshly grated nutmeg, to serve

Steam the cabbage strips over a pan of boiling water for about five minutes. Drain and transfer the slightly al dente strips to a warm bowl. Dot in the butter cubes and leave in a warm oven till you are ready to eat. Toss the cabbage and add a good grind of white pepper and some coarse sea salt, as well as fresh nutmeg at the table.

SAVOY CABBAGE
WITH LEEKS, BACON AND EGGS

I always think that a hearty bacon and egg brunch on a Saturday sets the tone for a relaxing weekend. This dish has the added bonus of a couple of healthy veg, so you don't have to feel guilty and can perhaps sneak in an extra treat or two before the day is through. The cabbage and bacon complement each other perfectly and when the egg is pierced and the hot yolk runs over them, a wonderful day is in the making. Use the whole cabbage, apart from the stalk: the tougher outer leaves pack plenty of flavour; they just need to be sliced more thinly than the paler leaves.

SERVES 4

300g streaky bacon, cut into 1cm squares, or lardons

2 large leeks, green tops only, washed and thinly sliced

1 large Savoy cabbage, stalk removed, cut into strips

4 free-range eggs

salt and freshly ground black pepper

crusty bread, to serve

Heat a heavy frying pan and drop in the bacon squares. Don't stir them around; leave them to crisp, although an occasional shake of the pan is fine. As they start to brown, toss in the leeks and, after a few minutes, the cabbage. Allow the cabbage to wilt before transferring the contents of the frying pan to a warmed bowl and covering it with foil. Poach an egg for every diner then serve by putting a mound of the cabbage, leeks and bacon on each plate, topped with the poached egg, a grind of black pepper and a crusty wedge of bread.

Variation: if you fancy something spicier for a mid-week dinner, try using hunks of chorizo instead of the bacon, and perhaps add a hint of chilli and garlic.

TWO-TONE CABBAGE STIR-FRY
WITH PRAWNS AND GINGER

This dish is good for the soul and I reckon the body does pretty well out of it too. Cabbage is comparatively high in vitamin C and folic acid, and chillies, ginger and garlic have cleansing properties, which means that a full fried breakfast the following morning will not seem so indulgent.

The trick with this dish – like any stir-fry – is speed. Slice the cabbage as thinly as possible and cook it extremely quickly so it still keeps bite. Prepare all the ingredients before you start cooking.

SERVES 4

10ml groundnut oil
1 red onion, thinly sliced
3 cloves garlic, thinly sliced
2 anchovies, finely chopped
2 small chillies, deseeded
   and thinly sliced
3cm piece root ginger, peeled
   and finely chopped

½ red cabbage, thinly sliced
½ Savoy cabbage, thinly sliced
250g raw prawns
20ml lemon juice
2 tablespoons fish sauce
250g rice noodles, soaked
   in boiling water to soften
2 tablespoons sesame oil

Heat the groundnut oil in a wok or heavy frying pan over a high heat until it spits. Add the chopped and sliced ingredients and the prawns and move them quickly around the pan. Reduce the heat and add the lemon juice and fish sauce. Drain the rice noodles and add to the mix. Cover immediately and leave to steam for about five minutes. Drizzle with the sesame oil and serve.

BREAST OF LAMB
WITH ONIONS AND RED CABBAGE

This is one of those dishes that looks after itself, requiring time but little effort. Resist the temptation to cook it quickly and it will reward you with the most tender meat, sweet onions, soft cabbage, succulent carrots and rich gravy. The gravy calls out for a dollop of mash; some misshapen rosemary roasties would fit the bill, too.

There may seem to be a lot of onions in this dish, but they melt down into a lovely velvety sauce, so are worth the tears. Besides, in the winter I like to find ways to use up my onion stockpile. Red or white onions are fine, but I find a mixture of the two works well. I suggest slicing all the onions thinly in a food processor.

SERVES 4–6

10ml vegetable oil

1 rolled lamb breast
(approx. 700g)

175ml glass red wine,
ideally Merlot

500g onions, thinly sliced

2 bay leaves

2 sticks celery, chopped

4 cloves garlic, chopped

200g baby Chantenay carrots,
whole

⅓ red cabbage, sliced

20ml red wine vinegar

salt and black pepper

Preheat the oven to 180°C/160°C fan/350°F/Gas mark 4. Heat the oil in a large frying pan. Season the lamb breast with salt and pepper and sear it all over in the hot pan until the outside is dark and semi-caramelised. Put the lamb to one side and deglaze the pan with the red wine, then pour the liquid into a large ovenproof dish. Put half the onions in the bottom of the pan with the bay leaves, celery and garlic. On top of this, pop in the whole baby carrots, followed by the cabbage. Nestle the lamb breast on top and smother it with the remaining onions. Put on a tight-fitting lid and pop into the oven for 40 minutes.

Reduce the oven temperature to 140°C/120°C fan/275°F/ Gas mark 1 and cook for a further 2 to 2½ hours. Remove the lamb and put it on a warm plate to rest. Pour off any liquid into a jug and discard the excess fat when it settles. Add the red wine vinegar to the liquid and reduce by a third in a saucepan over a medium heat. Ladle the mushy onions, cabbage and carrots into the centre of a serving plate. Cut the lamb into thick slices and arrange them on top, with a drizzle of the rich gravy.

PICKLED CABBAGE, WALNUT AND GOAT'S CHEESE SALAD

A winter salad needs to be hearty and rewarding. When it's too cold or too wet to venture beyond the front door, a ruby red cabbage is enough encouragement for me to batten down the hatches. The pickle flavour of the vinegar is not intense – it's more of a dressing – but the combination of the crunchy cabbage and walnuts with the soft cucumber and cheese make this a dish worth staying in for. Serve with a floury baked potato laden with butter.

SERVES 4

1 red cabbage, stalk removed, sliced into ribbons
1 large cucumber, diced
100ml white wine winegar
2 tablespoons Dijon mustard
100ml sunflower oil

50g capers
250g crumbly goat's cheese, cut into chunks
50g walnuts, coarsely chopped
salt

Put the cabbage and the cucumber in a deep bowl. Mix together the vinegar, mustard and oil. Season with a good pinch of salt and pour into the bowl. Leave the mixture to marinate in the fridge for as long as you can, tossing it from time to time to ensure an even coating – an hour is ideal. To serve, add the capers and sprinkle with generous chunks of the goat's cheese and walnuts.

Variation: if you don't like goat's cheese, substitute with hunks of creamy avocado and a sprinkling of torn basil leaves.

Cauliflower

Cauliflower is the kitchen equivalent of a cutaway in television. That is to say, a short shot that is cut into the main action to help tell the story, without being part of the main narrative. At its worst, a cutaway is visual wallpaper. Served on its own, cauli often doesn't stand up and shout enough on the plate. It needs a few mates with personality to stop it fading into nothingness. However, there are far too many extroverts and egos in this world for my liking, so I still like to have a row or two of caulis squeezed into the patch somewhere. They aren't exactly high maintenance.

In its defence, the cauliflower is much more of a team player. In the right company it is transformed into a really worthwhile ingredient. With strong flavours by its side, its modesty takes a back seat while its texture, robustness and willingness to absorb the qualities of those around it triumphs. In short, it's a good mixer. While it will never be the first up in the karaoke round, it cracks out some fantastic harmonies.

CURRY WITH CHICKPEAS AND CAULIFLOWER

Winter and curry are a fantastic marriage. Once the nights are cold and dark, curry becomes a regular craving for me and nothing else will do. Cauliflower works brilliantly in this hot and spicy sauce; it's almost as though it has been waiting patiently for curry night to kick in too. There's the added bonus that if you make enough, the next day it tastes even better.

SERVES 4

1 medium cauliflower, broken into medium florets

10ml groundnut oil

4 cloves garlic, finely chopped

5cm piece root ginger, finely chopped

2 small red chillies, deseeded and finely chopped

2 teaspoons cumin seeds

2 onions, chopped

1 large sweet potato, peeled and chopped

400g cooked chickpeas

2 teaspoons turmeric

300ml vegetable stock

400ml passata

75g fresh coriander, chopped

75g fresh mint, chopped, plus extra to garnish

juice 1 lime

150g plain yoghurt

30g almond flakes, toasted

salt

basmati rice, to serve

Boil the cauliflower florets in a saucepan of salted water for no more than five minutes, then drain (the florets should still be firm). Heat the oil in a large heavy-based frying pan over a medium heat. Add the garlic, ginger and chillies to the pan with the cumin seeds. Add the onions and sweet potato to the fragrant mixture along with the cauliflower and chickpeas. Sauté for a few minutes, stirring occasionally. Sprinkle over the turmeric and then add the stock. Bring to the boil and then reduce to a simmer. Add the passata, coriander and mint and simmer for ten more minutes.

Pour the lime juice over the curry, add a blob of yoghurt and a final fine sprinkling of mint plus the toasted almonds before serving on fluffy basmati rice. Bring on the cold and rain, it's warm inside.

Variation: this recipe is easily adapted, depending on the ingredients you have to hand. Butternut squash works just as well as the sweet potato and either potato or parsnip also go well with the cauliflower.

CAULIFLOWER CHEESE

Cauliflower is nothing if not versatile. It loves a strong spicy sauce, sitting wonderfully in a mind-blowing mid-week curry. Yet at the weekend it will happily languish in a cheese sauce and become a gentle, soft and comforting cauliflower cheese. With its rich, cheesy, velvet bath and slightly blistered brown topping it's a fantastic side with traditional roast beef. It delivers as a main course too. Everything hinges on decent cheese. Made with anything less than a strong Cheddar, this dish pales into insignificance. Adding fish to the dish might seem a bit weird, but it really works. No one will notice the anchovies, yet the cook appreciates the job they do as soon as the first mouthful hits the taste buds.

SERVES 2

1 medium cauliflower,
　broken into large florets
50g unsalted butter
2 tablespoons plain flour
500ml milk
1 bay leaf

1 tablespoon Dijon mustard.
200g mature Cheddar cheese,
　grated
150ml crème fraiche
4 anchovy fillets,
　finely chopped

Preheat the oven to 150°C/130°C fan/300°F/Gas mark 4. Partly cook the cauliflower florets in a saucepan of boiling salted water for five minutes. Drain them, return to the pan and cover with a lid.

Melt the butter over a low heat in a large saucepan. Stir in the flour to make a roux and cook gently for a few minutes. Turn up the heat and gradually add the milk, stirring continuously with a whisk to make a creamy sauce. Add the bay leaf and allow the sauce to thicken a little. Stir in the mustard and reduce the heat to low. Add the cheese and the crème fraiche and warm through.

Arrange the cauliflower florets in an ovenproof dish (or several smaller dishes for individual portions). Nestle the anchovies amongst the florets. Pour over the cheesy sauce and bake in the oven for 20–30 minutes. The rich sauce will start to blister and brown on top. Allow to cool for five minutes or so before serving.

Celeriac

....

With celeriac it's always worth remembering that you should not judge a book by its cover. When you picked up this one you may have been thinking, 'sophisticated, charming, aspirational and warm'. Celeriac faces the opposite predicament. If celeriac were a book you wouldn't pick it up at all, let alone give it to friends for Christmas. It would be the book that nobody wants, even on the last day of the closing down sale; even if it were completely free. In short, it doesn't have much going for it in the looks department. It has such thick gnarled skin that at times it resembles a rotting weed, abandoned in the soil. The longer the season goes on and the bigger it grows, the more ugly it becomes. In fact it doesn't blossom into anything attractive until you cook it. It's like a cross between celery and turnip I guess: just remember, it's what's inside that counts.

BAKED HONEY SALMON FILLET WITH CELERIAC PURÉE

The subtle flavours of the celeriac have a hint of bitterness that works brilliantly with the sweet, succulent fish in this dish. This is definitely comfort food for me. The ugly vegetable takes on a magnificence and sophistication that really defines the dish.

SERVES 4

4 salmon fillets

for the salmon marinade
30ml olive oil
1 tablespoon clear honey
4 teaspoons finely chopped dill
1 tablespoon Dijon mustard
10ml white wine vinegar

for the celeriac purée
1 celeriac (about 500g), peeled and cut into 3cm chunks
1 medium potato, peeled and cut into 3cm chunks
2 cloves garlic, peeled
50g unsalted butter
75ml double cream
salt
watercress, to serve

Put the salmon fillets in a shallow dish. Mix together the marinade ingredients then pour them over the salmon, ensuring that the fillets are fully coated. Cover and put in the fridge for at least two hours.

Preheat the oven to 200°C/180°C fan/400°F/Gas mark 6. Transfer the fillets to an ovenproof dish, baste with the marinade and bake for about 20 minutes.

Simmer the celeriac and potato chunks with the garlic in a large saucepan of salted water for about 20 minutes until soft. Drain and immediately put into a blender with the butter. Whizz until smooth. Gradually pour in the cream and keep blending until the purée reaches the right consistency. I prefer it to be thick enough to sit well on a plate, so it should not be too liquid, although looser than mash. Spoon the purée on to plates and set the salmon fillets on top. Serve with crisp, peppery watercress.

CELERIAC CHIPS WITH VENISON CUTLETS

Celeriac makes lovely chips or wedges: a crisp golden outside gives way to a wonderfully soft centre. The distinctive almost nutty flavour is a fantastic complement to venison, which also has a strong identity. The venison is best served slightly pink. Allow the chips to soak up the juices.

SERVES 4

1 celeriac, peeled and cut into thick chips or wedges
30ml olive oil
1 tablespoon Dijon mustard
2 cloves garlic
15 juniper berries
1 sprig thyme
juice ½ orange
30ml rapeseed oil
4 venison cutlets (approx 120g each)
salt and white pepper

Preheat the oven to 220°C/200°C fan/425°F/Gas mark 7. Boil the celeriac pieces in a saucepan of salted water for 8–10 minutes, then drain and pat dry. Transfer to a baking tray. Combine the olive oil and mustard and pour them over the chips. Mix with your hands to ensure that each chip is coated. Sprinkle with salt and pepper and put in the oven for half an hour, giving the tray a little shake from time to time.

In a pestle and mortar, crush the garlic cloves and juniper berries to a paste. Add the leaves from the thyme sprig, orange juice and rapeseed oil and mix together well. Pour over the venison cutlets and leave them to marinate at room temperature for 20 minutes, turning occasionally.

Heat a non-stick frying pan until it is very hot. Sear the cutlets on both sides for 3–4 minutes, then reduce the heat and cook for a further ten minutes, turning from time to time. Allow the cutlets to rest on a warm, covered plate for ten minutes before serving with the hot chips from the oven.

Leeks

······················

I do love leeks. There is such elegance in the way they grow so tall and straight. They are the last of the alliums to be harvested, and a true delight. Their subtle flavour makes them so versatile that they are constantly in demand. Before I grew them I used to systematically cut off the slightly fanned green top third and discard it. Now I strive to ensure minimal waste and I have realised that most of the time I only threw the top bit away because it was dirty (mud between the green layers) unlike the shiny white bit at the bottom. Pure laziness. I have now discovered a new system: washing the green bits! Not only do I waste less, I have also delighted in finding new ways to cook with them. Now I think I prefer the slightly more robust top leaves to the finer layers at the bottom; a bit like their spring onion cousins. What was I doing all those years?

LEEK TOPS WITH CHICKEN, WHITE WINE AND MUSTARD

This is a great dish for the day after you have roasted a chicken and steamed the white parts of the leeks to go with it. When you get home from work and all you have in the fridge is the leftover chicken and three or four green leek tops, don't despair: you are in for a treat!

SERVES 2

40g unsalted butter
300g green leek tops
   (tops of 2 large leeks),
   washed and thinly sliced

175ml dry white wine
250g cooked chicken, diced
1 tablespoon Dijon mustard
salt

Melt the butter in a saucepan and sauté the leek slices, sprinkling with a little salt. As they start to soften, pour in the glass of white wine and turn up the heat. Add the chicken and the Dijon mustard. Allow the liquid to reduce by half before transferring everything to a warm serving plate. If the white wine has been left over from the weekend, you have been very good. If it's from a new bottle you are being very bad. All told, it's worth having the day before just to have the day after.

CREAMED LEEKS WITH PARMESAN ON TOAST

Leeks may be a pretty humble vegetable, but they mix well with expensive friends to deliver a sophisticated dish. This is luxurious and feels almost naughty, particularly as I prefer it on toasted white bread: nice thick slices are best. The cream seeps through the crisp outer layer of the toast and makes the soft white chewy centre even more delicious.

SERVES 2

40g unsalted butter
2 medium leeks, washed and thinly sliced
1 tablespoon Dijon mustard
100ml double cream

30g Parmesan, grated
2 thick slices of crusty white bread
salt and freshly ground black pepper

Melt the butter in a heavy-based saucepan. Sprinkle the leek slices with salt and soften in the melted butter for about five minutes, stirring occasionally. Add the mustard and cream. Let the mixture bubble away gently for a further ten minutes before adding the Parmesan. Once the cheese melts, toast the bread, then spoon the creamy mixture onto the toast. Sprinkle with a grind of pepper and a final grating of Parmesan. Flash under the grill until the cheese forms a crust and tuck in while it's still hot.

LEEK, MUSHROOM AND BACON RISOTTO

Risotto was made for winter. It's such a satisfying dish to cook and can really ease the tension of a busy day. I would go so far as to say that it's mind-numbingly pleasurable to both prepare and eat. I'm practically reaching Zen just thinking about it.

SERVES 3–4

1 litre chicken stock
4 rashers smoked streaky bacon, chopped
2 leeks, washed and thinly sliced
150g unsalted butter

300g Arborio rice
175ml white wine
100g mushrooms, sliced
40g Parmesan, grated
drizzle truffle oil, to serve

Pour the stock into a saucepan and bring it to the boil. It's important that it is hot when it is added to the rice, so simmer it gently while you cook. Put a heavy based-pan on a medium to high heat and add the bacon pieces. When the fat starts to ooze from the bacon, add the leek tops (the green part) to the pan and stir. As the slices soften, reduce the heat, add half the butter and the remaining white parts of the leeks. Stir well and then add the rice, continuing to stir so that each grain is coated in buttery juices.

Pour in the white wine. As it reduces, ladle in a little hot stock. Keep the pan on a low to medium heat, stirring frequently. As each ladleful of stock is absorbed, add some more, but don't add too much stock at once. When two-thirds of the stock has been absorbed, add the mushrooms to the pan. When all the stock has been absorbed, turn off the heat. Add the Parmesan and serve with the tiniest drizzle of truffle oil.

PRAWN AND LEEK SPAGHETTI

I love dishes that can be turned round quickly and this requires barely longer than the time it takes to cook the pasta and pour the rosé. The leeks absorb the other flavours but still let you know they're there.

SERVES 2

150g spaghetti
50g unsalted butter
2 cloves garlic, finely chopped
4 medium leeks, washed and finely chopped
250g raw prawns

juice 1 unwaxed lemon, plus zest, to serve
1 teaspoon fennel seeds, ground
2 teaspoons paprika
salt and black pepper

Cook the spaghetti in a large saucepan of boiling, salted water according to the packet instructions, then drain, keeping a cupful of the water. Melt the butter in a heavy-based saucepan and add the garlic and leeks. Stir regularly until the leeks begin to soften. Add the prawns, the pasta water and the lemon juice. Turn up the heat. Sprinkle the ground fennel seeds into the pan with the paprika. Cover for five minutes until the prawns are cooked through. Add the spaghetti to the pan before serving and finish with a little lemon zest and black pepper.

Variation: for grown-up palates, a splash of aniseed liqueur added alongside the fennel seeds adds an extra kick.

PORK FILLET STUFFED WITH DATES AND LEEKS

This is like a huge pork, leek and apple sausage, but uses dates instead of apples. Unlike a sausage, it looks sophisticated and important, especially when carved at the table. Guests will utter 'wow' or 'yum' as it reveals itself to be a type of roulade and definitely not just a sausage. You need to transform the round pork tenderloin into a butterflied thin rectangle of meat. To do this, use a very sharp knife to make an incision about a centimetre deep from top to bottom along the length of one side of the loin. Open out the cut with your fingers and make another cut into the thickness of the flesh. Continue cutting until you have effectively 'unrolled' the fillet. A butcher might do this for you if you ask extremely nicely.

SERVES 4

1 tablespoon Dijon mustard
1 pork tenderloin
   (approx. 600g), butterflied,
   offcuts diced finely
1 medium leek (approx. 100g),
   roughly chopped

80g pitted dates,
   roughly chopped
50g unsalted butter, cubed
6 rashers smoked streaky
   bacon
20ml cider vinegar

Preheat the oven to 190°C/170°C fan/375°F/Gas mark 5. Spread the mustard over the inside of the meat. Mix together the leek, dates and diced pork and spread them evenly along the length. Dot the butter on top. Carefully roll up the pork: you may need cocktail sticks to hold it together, as it will bulge. Lay the bacon rashers diagonally across a board and roll the stuffed pork so that the rashers completely cover it, like the skin on a sausage. Put the pork in a roasting tin and cook in the oven for 35 minutes.

Allow the meat to rest before serving. Deglaze the roasting tin with the cider vinegar and some water, to make a gravy. Serve with mashed potato and wilted buttery spinach.

MUSSELS WITH CIDER AND LEEKS

Eating mussels always turns a meal into an occasion. There's a sense of theatre in scooping up the juices in a half shell or dunking the crusty bread. The pile of discarded shells in the bowl (very useful on the compost heap I must add) are like a trophy, testament to the endeavours of the diners. Yet, mussels are a simple, quick and easy dish to prepare. Follow the health warnings and discard the broken ones and those that don't close when they are tapped (or decline to open when they are cooked). This dish is a joy: I love to make it with my early leek harvest, when the leeks are small, yet bursting with the flavour that is tightly packed into the stems.

SERVES 2

4 rashers streaky bacon, cut into slivers

10ml olive oil

4 small leeks, cut into 5cm long rings

4 cloves garlic, finely chopped

1 bay leaf

250ml dry cider

300g prepared mussels

200ml single cream

20g chopped flat-leaf parsley, to serve

crusty bread, to serve

Put the bacon with the olive oil in a large, heavy-based pan over a medium heat. Add the leeks, garlic and bay leaf and allow the fat from the bacon to coat the leeks. As they colour, pour in the cider, turn up the heat and cover the pan. Give the mussels a final rinse under cold water, then tip them into the steaming broth. Cover, so the mussels open in the steam. After no more than five minutes, lower the heat and pour in the cream. Warm through and sprinkle with chopped parsley. Serve with the crusty bread.

LEEK AND POTATO SOUP

Soup is a great leveller. It doesn't matter how dishevelled and war-torn a pile of spuds and a handful of leeks might appear, by the time they are cooked nobody will know. That is the art of the cook: transforming the mundane into a dish so delicious and elegant that everyone will wish you had made more. Some soups have a place on the table at any time of year. Others have their seasonal moment. I know it's winter when I make this soup. It's warm, hearty and infinitely satisfying – and just wouldn't be the same in any other season.

SERVES 2–4

3 leeks, washed and
   sliced lengthways
40g unsalted butter
500g potatoes, peeled and
   cut into bite-sized chunks
2 cloves garlic, thinly sliced
800ml vegetable stock

1 bay leaf
10ml olive oil
100–300ml vegetable or
   rapeseed oil, for deep frying
4 slices Parma ham
150ml double cream
salt and pepper

Put half a leek to one side, melt the butter in a heavy-based saucepan and sauté the rest of the leeks with the potato chunks and garlic for a few minutes. Add the stock and bay leaf and bring to the boil. Cover the saucepan and simmer for 15 minutes until the potatoes are soft.

Use a slotted spoon to remove a spoonful or two of the potatoes. Allow the liquid to drain off and pat them dry with kitchen paper. Put them in a small ovenproof dish, drizzle with the olive oil, sprinkle with salt and pepper and pop under a hot grill for about ten minutes to colour.

Remove the bay leaf, then pour the soup into a blender and blitz to a smooth liquid. Return the soup to the saucepan. Slice the remaining leek lengthways into very fine ribbons or shreds. Heat a heavy-based saucepan or deep fat fryer and pour in oil to a depth of 1cm. When the oil is extremely hot, drop in the strands of leek. Don't overcrowd the pan; cook a few at a time. The timing is critical: you need to fish them out as soon as they begin to colour so they don't burn (30 seconds can make a difference). Drain the leek strands on kitchen paper and pop the Parma ham under the grill for a few minutes until it is crisp.

Before serving, pour the cream into the soup and warm it through. Pour the soup into warmed bowls, arrange a flotilla of roasted potato pieces in the middle of each, scrunch over a sprinkle of toasted Parma ham and top with a nest of leek strands.

CHICKEN, LEEK AND MUSHROOM PIE WITH SPINACH AND CARROTS

We do not truly hibernate, though sometimes it seems like a nice idea. This is a dish for those winter days when you can feel the cold in your bones and you just want to huddle down by an open fire with a pie and a movie. However, when I decide to serve this pie with spinach, I still have to venture into the meteorological misery of the great outdoors to pick it before I can enjoy the warmth of the kitchen and lounge.

Such weather makes me appreciate the vegetables that are hanging on out there even more. They are like the friends who stay around at the end of a party to clear up. Dependable. This is also a time when appearance is less important. The spinach looks particularly ragged; a few holes here and there and large irregular leaves. Within that well-worn exterior is immense flavour but it would be easy to just walk by, if you were simply judging by appearance. Actually there is still plenty to eat on the allotment: some culinary treats, such as carrots and parsnips, are hiding beneath the soil, the beetroots are doing their best to push out of the ground and the cabbages and kale are waiting to be harvested. The leeks, no longer growing upright, lean over in the wind, hoping to be pulled from the ground. Today the carrots, spinach and leeks get the nod.

When you cook the carrots, boil them ferociously over a high heat until the water all but disappears and then let them start to caramelise in the butter. Don't burn the saucepan, but be brave enough to let them colour. By this time of year it's hard to know where the spinach leaves end and the stalks begin. It's not an easy job separating them, so rather than try, just leave them as they are. Once they are washed, chop them up finely and steam them. Truffle oil may be expensive, but a small hint of this earthy oil really transforms this dish.

for the pastry
110g unsalted butter, cubed
200g plain flour, plus 20g for rolling
3 tablespoons water
1 egg, beaten, to glaze
salt

for the filling
300ml milk
20g dried porcini mushrooms
40g unsalted butter
30g flour
300g chicken breast or deboned leg, cut into bite-sized pieces
1 large leek, washed, sliced into finger-length ribbons
4 cloves garlic, chopped
125g field mushrooms, sliced

1 tablespoon Dijon mustard
1 teaspoon truffle oil
250g carrots, thinly sliced diagonally
knob butter, plus extra for garnishing
1 bay leaf
100g spinach leaves, washed and finely chopped
salt

First make the pastry. The trick to good pastry is not to overwork it. Rub the cold butter, flour and salt through your fingers to make breadcrumbs, then stir in the water and form a ball of dough. Cover in clingfilm and pop in the fridge for half an hour. Alternatively, making pastry in a food processor is even easier: pulse the butter, flour and salt until you get the breadcrumbs and slowly add the water, pulsing as you go.

Heat the milk in a saucepan, but turn off the heat before it comes to a simmer. Add the mushrooms and allow them to soak until the milk cools. Preheat the oven to 200°C/ 180°C fan/400°F/Gas mark 6. Strain the milk into a jug and put the porcini to one side. Melt the butter in another saucepan and stir in the flour to make a roux, adding a little of the flavoured milk. Gradually add the rest of the milk, keeping the heat low and stirring until all the milk is added.

Arrange the chicken pieces, leeks, garlic and field mushrooms with the porcini in a pie dish with a pie funnel in the middle. Random is the word of the day here, so that there is variety in every portion. Stir the mustard and truffle oil into the sauce and pour it over the top.

Roll out the pastry on a floured board and lay it over the pie dish. Prick a couple of holes in the centre, and trim the edges, allowing enough to crimp with a forefinger and thumb all round. Make some shapes from the leftover pastry to decorate the top. Glaze with beaten egg and put in the oven for 40 minutes.

Ten minutes before the pie is ready, put the carrots in a large saucepan with a generous knob of butter. Add water (not enough to cover, just a tad less), the bay leaf and a pinch of salt. Cover and bring to the boil quickly, shaking the saucepan occasionally. Cook for about eight minutes: you can add more butter and water, if necessary. Steam the spinach for five minutes in the steamer so the leaves wilt and the stems retain some crunch. Top with a drizzle of melted butter.

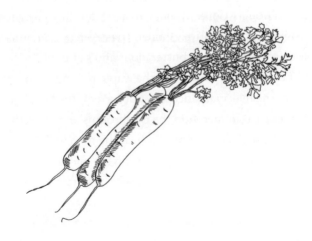

Sprouts, kale and hardy greens

....

If I hadn't grown them, I would have been quite happy never to have seen a sprout again after childhood. Even if they had been on the edge of extinction, I would have just thought, 'Darwin was right: evolution, natural selection: sprouts are boring – live without them.'

The trouble is, I got a free packet of sprout seeds on the front of a gardening magazine. I kept them for two years and was about to throw them out when I noticed that I had a spare seed tray. So I planted a few and put them in the corner of the greenhouse. It was the start of a wonderful friendship. Five years on, the sprouts have pride of place every winter.

Kale really thrives in the winter and shares the same bed as the sprouts. It is so green, so healthy looking and hardy that it is definitely one of nature's survivors. It just loves to grow. I reckon that if a plant is that robust and belligerent, it must be given a chance to shine in the kitchen. It has incredible flavour; a strong, perhaps acquired, taste, but one I have grown to love in recent years.

SPROUTS, APPLES AND BACON

The flavour of the tightly packed leaves of a young sprout is so intense that it can stand up to pretty strong competition on the plate. Pork and cabbage is a trusted combination and this duo work particularly well together. They are both enhanced by apple. Old sprouts are best avoided: they bore for Britain. These are my luxury sprouts: the addition of butter and cream is naughty, especially with the bacon fat, but somehow they elevate the dish so it becomes a treat.

SERVES 2, OR 4 AS A SIDE

200g smoked fatty streaky bacon, diced

200g sprouts, trimmed and halved

100ml dry cider

100ml vegetable stock

2 tablespoons mustard

50g unsalted butter

3 eating apples, peeled and thickly sliced

20ml Calvados

100ml cream

freshly ground black pepper

50g flaked almonds, toasted, to serve

Put a large non-stick saucepan over high heat and add the bacon; it will crisp in its own fat. When it starts to sizzle, add the sprouts cut side down, and cook for a couple of minutes, so they take on some colour. Reduce the heat and add the cider, stock, mustard and butter. Simmer gently until most of the liquid disappears. Don't overcook the sprouts – it's better to keep them on the firm side.

Put the apple slices in the pan and pour over the Calvados. Carefully burn off the alcohol by igniting the Calvados, tilting the pan to catch the flame. Reduce the heat to low before adding the cream. Let the sauce bubble away for about five minutes while the apple slices soften. Serve sprinkled with the toasted almonds and be generous with the black pepper mill.

WHITING WITH CHORIZO AND SPICY KALE

The flavour of the combined kale and chorizo in this dish is really intense. The whiting works wonderfully and is soft and delicate by comparison. This is a quick dish and one you will come back to time and time again.

SERVES 2

30g unsalted butter
100g chorizo, cubed
100g kale, washed
   and roughly chopped

2 whiting fillets,
   approx. 150g each
20ml lemon juice
freshly ground black pepper

Melt the butter in a heavy-based saucepan and add the chorizo; the paprika and oil from the spicy sausage will start to melt into the butter. Add the kale, put the whiting fillets on top, sprinkle them with lemon juice and cover the pan. The fish will steam in about 6–7 minutes – don't cook for longer or it will go to mush. Serve with a grind of black pepper.

CHRISTMAS BURGER
WITH BUBBLE AND SQUEAK PATTIES

I like to make these burgers as soon as the Christmas decorations go up. I see it as a little sneak preview of the flavours to come; a 'getting in the mood' dish. Thankfully this early in the season, the words 'turkey' and 'using up' haven't yet been considered in the same sentence. The poultry adventure is still fresh and – dare I say – exciting. It's a fitting way to start the season of indulgence and joy.

SERVES 4–6

500g parsnips, cut into 1cm thick chips

20ml olive oil

1 large red onion, finely chopped

2 cloves garlic, finely chopped

100g breadcrumbs

150g chestnut purée

80g dates, finely chopped

400g turkey mince

4 rashers smoked bacon, finely chopped

1 egg, beaten

flour, for dusting

50g sprouts, finely chopped

70g unsalted butter

100g mashed potato

cranberry jelly, to serve

20g flaked almonds, toasted, to serve

Preheat the oven to 200°C/180°C fan/400°F/Gas mark 6. Put the parsnip chips and oil in a roasting tin and cook in the oven for 30 minutes.

Mix the onions and garlic in a large bowl, along with the breadcrumbs, chestnut purée, dates and turkey mince. Add the bacon to the mix with the beaten egg. Mix thoroughly; hands are best for this. Shape the mixture into burgers, give each a dusting of plain flour and grill for about eight minutes on each side.

Put a frying pan over a medium heat and soften the sprouts in 50g of the butter. When they are soft, remove them and mix with the mashed potato in a bowl. Mix thoroughly and form small patties. Put the patties in the frying pan with the rest of the butter and cook so that both sides have a caramelised skin.

Serve the turkey burger on top of the bubble and squeak patty, with a generous dollop of cranberry sauce, a shower of toasted almonds and the parsnip chips on the side.

Variation: you can adapt this recipe to mark the end of the festivities too. Replace the turkey mince with roughly chopped turkey leftovers and use diced ham instead of the bacon. You can hide all sorts of leftovers in the bubble and squeak patties – or the burgers for that matter.

Swedes, turnips and parsnips

I have to admit that when I sit ordering seeds neither turnips nor swedes are at the top of my list. They aren't glamorous and 'must have' compared with the summer crops. I don't leave room for a huge turnip or swede patch either. They fall into the 'I ought to plant a few' category. But when I harvest them, I am so glad that I have found them a place. They have wonderful flavour and are a really welcome winter vegetable. They also store well.

As for parsnips, I plan for many and never seem to grow enough. As a result I hold them in great reverence and always make sure that I keep some for Christmas.

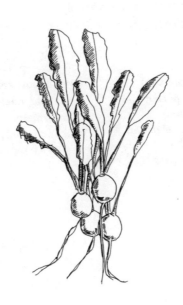

HAGGIS, CREAMED POTATO AND BASHED NEEPS WITH WHISKY SAUCE

My favourite haggis memory (not that I have many) is from Edinburgh. A small pub not far from the castle wasn't what I had in mind for a gourmet lunch before catching an afternoon flight. However, it was raining ridiculously hard and the light from the pub spilled onto the dark, shiny pavement, even at midday. I couldn't resist going in. I had intended to order a quick beer before heading out to the wintry streets to find a restaurant. Then the lightning flashed outside. I made the executive decision to stay in the pub and resigned myself to what I expected would be standard pub fare. I was wrong. The haggis, tatties and neeps were more than warming. The spicy and sensational food and the compulsory drams of whisky made me forget about the weather and almost miss my flight. That would have taken some explaining.

Despite its unglamorous ingredients, serving haggis always feels like a treat to me and elevates potato and swede to gourmet magnificence. My whisky sauce in the pub came neat in a glass, but I've refined it for southern softies. A dram or two of neat whisky helps cut through the fat and so allegedly reduces the chances of high cholesterol. Worth a try, if just for health reasons.

SERVES 4

1 haggis (approx. 500g)

1.5kg potatoes, peeled and
    cut into chunks

1 large swede, peeled and
    cut into chunks

100g unsalted butter

20ml double cream, optional

4 shallots, finely chopped

30ml whisky

salt and freshly ground
    black pepper

Bring a large saucepan of water to the boil. Reduce to a simmer and pop in the haggis. Cook according to the packet instructions. Meanwhile, put the potatoes in another saucepan of salted water and bring to the boil, and cook the swede in a third saucepan. When the potatoes are cooked, drain them and add half the butter and the cream before mashing to a lumpless mound. Drain the cooked swede and bash with the back of a fork, retaining some texture. Add most of the remaining butter and a good grind of black pepper.

Heat a heavy-based saucepan and sauté the shallots in the remaining butter. Add the whisky and burn off the alcohol. Drizzle sparsely on the side of the plate. Serve the neeps (swedes) on the tatties and put the haggis on top.

TURNIPS AND LARDONS

Turnips are so robust in both flavour and structure that they don't always spring to mind when you need a delicate comforting treat. This dish keeps its flavour but brings out a whole new side to the turnips' character. With a crisp, caramelised outer layer and soft, chewy centre the sweet turnip melts beside the crisp, salty bacon. The creamy sauce makes it sublime.

SERVES 4 as a side, perhaps for Christmas lunch

40g unsalted butter

4 small turnips, peeled, diced in 1cm cubes

200ml water

200g smoked lardons

175ml dry white wine

100ml double cream

20g chopped flat-leaf parsley

Melt the butter in a heavy-based saucepan and add the turnips. Cook over a high heat for a couple of minutes, then add the water. Continue cooking over a high heat until nearly all the liquid has evaporated and the turnips start to caramelise. Reduce the heat to medium and add the lardons. Allow them to crisp, then add the wine and scrape up all the bits that have stuck to the bottom of the pan. Reduce to the lowest heat. Pour in the cream and sprinkle with the finely chopped parsley.

WINTER CHICKEN CASSEROLE

It's easy to feel shortchanged by a winter's night. Somehow a summer evening (sitting out with a glass of wine, watching the sun disappear) seems last longer. In winter, by the time you have reached home, cooked and eaten it's almost time to think about bed. Recently I have endeavoured to beat this illusion by having hot food ready for the moment I set foot in the door. When you leave the darkness of the street behind you and breathe in the warming sweet smells emanating from the oven, the winter's nights suddenly come alive again.

I've discovered just how tasty and economical chicken thighs are in the winter. They have plenty of meat on them and suit this dish wonderfully. The root vegetables benefit from a long slow cook, so this dish bubbles happily away while I am at work, just waiting to greet me when I get home. If you like to plan ahead, you could make enough to last for two or three nights. I usually prefer to cook from scratch, but it's great to have a few bowls of this to look forward to when stuck in commuter traffic with the wipers on overdrive.

SERVES 4–6

6 large carrots,
   chopped into 2–3cm chunks
1 medium turnip,
   chopped into 2–3cm chunks
½ swede,
   chopped into 2–3cm chunks
4 large parsnips,
   chopped into 2–3cm chunks
1 large leek, washed and sliced

500g button mushrooms,
   sliced
1kg chicken thighs
2 bay leaves
4 cloves garlic,
   whole and unpeeled
1 litre vegetable stock
75ml white wine vinegar

Put two-thirds of the vegetables into an ovenproof dish with a lid. Lay the chicken thighs on top, then cover with the remaining vegetables. Pop in the bay leaves and garlic cloves, then add the stock and white wine vinegar. Cover and set the oven to come on about two hours before you are due home. The trick is to cook this dish very slowly at a low temperature for two hours minimum at 170°C/150°C fan/335°F/Gas mark 3. When served, the chicken will fall off the bone and the vegetables melt.

SPICY PARSNIP ROSTI WITH CHILLI SAUCE

For perfection this dish should be made with the fine strands of parsnip that only a mandoline can produce, but a grater will also work, if you feel your fingers are in danger when using a mandoline. The parsnip flavour really sings with the chilli sauce.

SERVES 4 AS A STARTER

for the fritters
- 1 egg, beaten
- 2 teaspoons each turmeric, chilli powder and cumin
- 150g plain yoghurt
- 50g plain flour
- 1 large onion, finely chopped
- 4 cloves garlic, finely chopped
- 500g parsnips, peeled and cut into fine strips
- olive oil, for frying
- salt and pepper

for the chilli sauce
- 3 red chillies, deseeded
- 150ml passata
- 20ml lime juice
- 20ml vegetable oil

Mix the egg, spices, yoghurt and flour in a bowl. Add the onion, garlic and parsnip strips. Mix well. Squeeze the mixture into burgers and fry in hot oil in a heavy-based frying pan until they are golden on both sides. Reduce the heat, cover the pan and continue to cook through, turning occasionally.

For the sauce, put the chillies and other ingredients in a food processor and blitz until smooth. Serve with the hot parsnip cakes.

HONEY AND CUMIN PARSNIPS

If I had to choose between them, I'd rather forfeit the turkey on Christmas Day than an extra bowl of these. The parsnips are soft and squidgy and wonderfully sweet. The cumin adds a depth of flavour and gives off an aroma that fills the kitchen and alerts the taste buds in anticipation of the meal to come.

SERVES 2

1 tablespoon clear honey
10ml rapeseed oil
20ml white wine vinegar
500g parsnips, cut into
   even-sized chunks

30g unsalted butter
2 teaspoons cumin seeds
sea salt

Preheat the oven to 220°C/200°C fan/425°F/Gas mark 7. Mix together the honey, oil and white wine vinegar into a sticky paste. Coat the parsnips thoroughly in the mixture before transferring them to an ovenproof dish. Keep any excess mixture to one side. Put the parsnips in the oven for 20 minutes.

Turn them and drizzle the leftover mixture over them, then add the butter and sprinkle over the cumin seeds. Give a final mix and pop back into the oven for a further 15 minutes. When the parsnips are soft on the inside and candied on the outside, they are ready.

WINTER ROAST CHICKEN WITH ROASTIE ROOTIES

I make no apologies for including roast chicken twice in this book. This recipe offers a very different experience from its summer cousin. Both dishes reflect their respective seasons and somehow encapsulate the moment too. Once you fully appreciate this, it becomes clear just how the seasons affect our moods and rituals. The summer chicken is based on lemons and has zest and vitality, whereas the winter bird is caressed by hardy warm and comforting vegetables. This roast will bolster you through the cold and dark days. That for me is why eating seasonally, or as seasonally as possible, is balm for the soul, as well as just what the doctor ordered. However big the table and however sprawling the family, a good hearty winter roast will always make the home a happy one.

When preparing the roast vegetables, size is important. Some vegetables require longer cooking than others, so adjust the size of the chunks accordingly. Harder veg, such as beetroot, should be cut into smaller chunks than the softer parsnips, for example.

SERVES 4–6

for the chicken

1 chicken (2kg)
3 carrots, 1 chopped, 2 whole
1 leek, washed and chopped
1 stick celery, chopped,
  plus a few leaves (optional)
3 onions, 1 chopped,
  2 quartered
3 sprigs thyme

3 cloves garlic, chopped
1 bay leaf
30g unsalted butter
vegetable oil, for drizzling
175ml red wine
175ml water
salt

for the roast rooties

selection of parsnips, carrots, beetroots, squash, potatoes,
  turnips, peeled and cut into chunks
30ml vegetable oil
salt

broccoli or cabbage, to serve

Preheat the oven to 200°C/180°C fan/400°F/Gas mark 6. Fill the chicken cavity with the chopped carrots, leeks, celery, chopped onion and thyme. Add the celery leaves, garlic, bay leaf and butter.

Rub a drizzle of vegetable oil over the outside of the bird and sprinkle it with salt. Put it in a small roasting tin, just big enough to hold the chicken, on top of the quartered onions and the whole carrots. Pour over the wine and water. The bird should hover above the liquid. As it cooks, the juices from the bird and the softening onions and carrot will make a fantastic base for the gravy.

Roast the chicken for 1½ hours. After half an hour put the roasting vegetables into the biggest roasting tin you can fit on the oven shelf. It's best if there is space for everything spread out, rather than piled up, so use two tins if necessary. Drizzle the vegetables with oil, sprinkle on some salt and give the tin a good shake before putting it in the oven.

When they are cooked, transfer the chicken and vegetables to warmed serving dishes, while you concentrate on the gravy and steam some greens. Cook the broccoli or cabbage stalks in a pan of boiling water before steaming the rest, to give you some top-up liquid for the gravy.

Deglaze the roasted vegetable pan with a little of the vegetable water and mix this in with the onion-flavoured juices from the chicken roasting tin. Dilute with as much vegetable water as you need, then strain into a jug. Allow the gravy to settle for a few minutes and carefully pour off the layer of oil on the surface.

A new day, a new dawn:
it's starting to feel good again...

Even in the greyest, coldest, shortest days of winter a vegetable grower is never too far from summer. That's how I look at it anyway (and life, to be honest). It would be easy to complain about the January cold that seeps into the bones, or the gloom that at first glance appears to be all that is left after Christmas. Yet to indulge in such melancholic despair would be to miss the point. Nature may have slowed down, but it hasn't stopped. The gardener only has time to take a deep breath before the cycle starts again.

I love to turn over the soil on crisp days and wait for the frosts to break down the sods into a fine crumb. Freeing a patch of earth from persistent perennial weeds is also a joy on the right days: these are the days when no one else is around, when the robin hops eagerly in the shadows looking for lunch and a hot flask of tea is a simple pleasure.

It would be a cliché to evangelise about growing your own vegetables and claim that doing this is better for you than placing an Internet grocery order. There's no proof. All I know is that since I have made the effort, I enjoy cooking and eating in a way I never experienced before. I appreciate ingredients more profoundly and find ways to use them efficiently.

It seems to me that we have made our lives complicated. We have let accountants and bankers monopolise us; multinational corporations and marketing geniuses sell us lifestyles we can hardly afford and we continually run to just keep up with ourselves. Life can be simple. Planting some seeds, watching them grow and eating the results is fundamental. Trust me, it's also fun – sometimes. As the year comes to an end and New Year dawns, it's comforting to know that whatever the future holds for us, we can still grow rocket. When you have a spade in your hand, there's always something to look forward to.

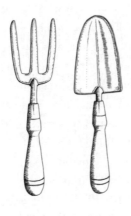

Acknowledgements

I must first thank the love of my life, Natasha, for supporting me in everything I do. She is forever patient and spurs me on every day. Freddie also deserves my praise. Not least for indulging me when I spend so many hours on the plot. The fact that he can tell courgettes from pumpkins and runners from broads fills me with immense pride. He will grow into a fine specimen, I'm sure. His kid brother Ted cannot yet wield a wheelbarrow. That time will come as he follows along behind me planting and harvesting (there is little in between of interest to a child) and I look forward to the memories we will create together.

In addition, I would like to thank my departed parents. With out them, of course none of this would have been possible. Full stop. Biology aside, they gave me just enough of everything to help me become who I am. I'm sure, in so many ways, they would have loved to have given me more. I am ever thankful that I wasn't given so much that I took anything for granted.

At Orion Publishing, Amanda Harris deserves my heart-felt thanks. Giving me the opportunity to write this book is something for which I shall always be grateful. Thanks also to Tamsin English and Kate Wanwimolruk, my editors, and Mary-Jane Wilkins, for making sense of it all.

In the food world, I have been fortunate to work with exceptional and inspiring cooks and chefs: Nigel Slater, Nigella Lawson, Michel Roux Jnr., Lorraine Pascale, The Hairy Bikers, James Martin, Rachel Khoo and many others. They have all been generous with their patience, trust, friendship and expertise and made my day job an absolute joy.

Of course for every person on screen there is an army of people behind the scenes. My programme teams work tirelessly to create stunning, screen-lickingly beautiful programmes. Jenny Fazey, Michelle Crowley, Karen Plumb, Maria Norman, Michelle Soldani,

Dulcie Arnold, Hannah Corneck, Emma Boswell, Will Knott, Richard Hill, Amy Joyce, Simon Knight, Dom Cyriax and all the editors, crews, production teams and home economists who always deliver. Thank you for sweating for hours over which shots of an onion to use and how to make a lettuce look good – geniuses.

Finally, I would like to acknowledge those who trusted me to make TV programmes in the first place: Jay Hunt, Danny Cohen, Janice Hadlow, Alison Kirkham, Charlotte Moore, Tracy Forsyth, Carla-Maria Lawson, Lindsay Bradbury, Damian Kavanagh, Emma Swain, Liam Keelan, Dan McGolpin, William Miller, Kalpna Woolf and Tom Archer. Thank you for the opportunities.

It's funny how life goes. I used to think my dad was a bit crazy persevering with his radishes under the washing line – but now, it all makes sense. At least to me.

About the author

Pete Lawrence is an award-winning executive producer, writer and creative director in television. He has a varied portfolio of work ranging from documentaries to feature programmes, including drama and studio work, but in recent years he has been a driving force in television food programming.

Pete's name is behind some of the world's most popular food series and he has worked with the very best in the business, including Nigel Slater, Nigella Lawson, Michel Roux Jnr., Lorraine Pascale, The Hairy Bikers, James Martin and Rachel Khoo.

In his spare time Pete seeks solace on his allotment and writes about his ongoing relationships with the seasons, nature and his produce, creating mouthwatering dishes from the fruits of his labours.

Pete gained a first class BA (Hons) in film-making before embarking on a career in television.

Follow Pete at 🐦@digthisfood

Index